July 7, 2015

Bassett Virginia

For Betty Willard,

At Bassett, Virginia Train Station,

Enjoy!

LHP

Also By Thomas D. Perry

Henry County Heritage Book Volume One

Fieldale Virginia

Beyond Mayberry: Andy Griffith and Mount Airy NC

The Possum That Crossed The Road

Ascent To Glory: The Genealogy of J. E. B. Stuart

The Graham Mansion: A History

Ghosts of the Graham Mansion

The Free State Of Patrick: Patrick County Virginia In The Civil War

J. E. B. Stuart's Birthplace: The History of the Laurel Hill Farm

God's Will Be Done: The Christian Life of J. E. B. Stuart

Images of America: Henry County Virginia

Images of Patrick County Virginia: Postcards

Martinsville, Virginia

Mount Airy, North Carolina

Patrick County Virginia: Then and Now

Patrick County Oral History Project: A Guide

J. E. B. Stuart's Birthplace: A Guide

A Dinky Railroad

Civil War Stories From Surry County NC

Visit www.freestateofpatrick.com for more information.

Bassett Virginia

History and Memory Series of Laurel Hill Publishing

By Thomas D. Perry

Copyright 2014 Laurel Hill Publishing LLC

ISBN-13: 978-1456349943
ISBN-10: 1456349945

Laurel Hill Publishing
P. O. Box 11
4443 Ararat Highway
Ararat, VA 24053
www.freestateofpatrick.com
freestateofpatrick@yahoo.com
276-692-5300

On the title page are the John D. Bassett High School Varsity Cheerleaders during the 1970 Bassett Christmas Parade. In the front row from left to right are Lynne Joyce '71, Pam Akers '71, Carol Anthony '72, and blocked is Myra Terry '71 (Captain). In the back row are Clarke Stanley '72, (Co-Captain) Vickie Price 72', Betsy White '72, Genette Hite '72, and sitting directly behind but blocked is Cindy Fulcher '71. In 2009, Ward Armstrong found a car identical to the one in the parade and we got several of my "Covergirls" together to reenact their famous photo in front of their high school.

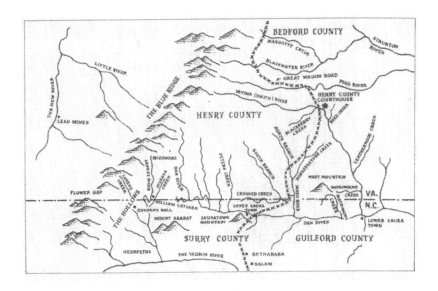

Formed in 1777, Henry County once contained the land from modern day Carroll, Franklin, and Patrick Counties extending west along the North Carolina and Virginia dividing line beyond where the Appalachian Mountains cross the line surveyed by groups including William Byrd and Peter Jefferson.

For Bobbi

"To our mothers, we owe our highest esteem, for it is from their gift of life that the flow of events begins that shapes our destiny."
Ronald Reagan, April 6, 1983

The Great Wagon Road travels from Market Street along the Delaware River in Philadelphia, Pennsylvania, to the banks of the Savannah River in Augusta, Georgia, via Henry County, Virginia. An old Indian Trail it parallels Highway 220 near Bassett, Virginia.

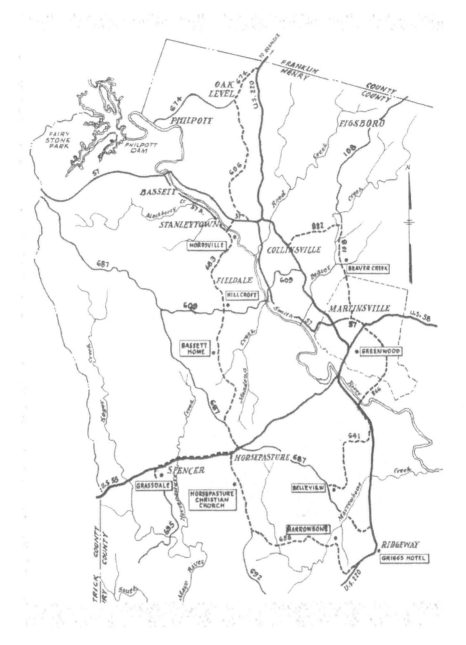

This book covers the northwest section of Henry County, west of Route 220 and north of the Smith River including Stanleytown, Philpott, and Bassett.

David Wright went to John D. Bassett High School Class of 1960 and now he owns it as part of his company, EMI Imaging. Well known for his community involvement from the Henry County Food Pantry, Building Fund of the Bassett Historical Center and hosting the Bassett Heritage Festival in September 2014. David takes his Christian faith seriously and helps his fellow man. For his support over the years, this author wanted to make special mention of David.

Dr. John Bing and others worked to have this Virginia Highway Historical Marker placed along Highway 57 near the intersection with Bypass Highway 220.

This Virginia Historical Highway Marker denotes Fort Trial built in 1756 during the French and Indian War as a barrier to Indian attacks. George Washington visited here as a young officer in the Virginia Militia.

Contents

Introduction	15
Elva's Chapter	19
Bassett Furniture Company	31
Bassett Folks	59
Smith River	83
Train, Train	99
School Days	109
Around Bassett	137
Hogue and Joyce Craig	167
Unknown Bassett	173
Blue Ridge Hardware and Supply Company	177
More Bassett Images	179
Newspaper Clippings	195
Trent Furniture Company	211
Philpott, People, Politicians....	215
Fon's Grocery	241
More Folks In Bassett	245
From The Pages Of Books	265
Photos Via Email	273
Hearth and Home	291
Bassett Historical Center	299
Index	333
About The Author	339

"It was the best of times, it was the worst of times, it was the age of wisdom, it was the age of foolishness, it was the epoch of belief, it was the epoch of incredulity, it was the season of Light, it was the season of Darkness, it was the spring of hope, it was the winter of despair, we had everything before us, we had nothing before us, we were all going direct to Heaven, we were all going direct the other way – in short, the period was so far like the present period, that some of its noisiest authorities insisted on its being received, for good or for evil, in the superlative degree of comparison only."

Charles Dickens, *A Tale of Two Cities*

Introduction
Images of Henry County

I first came to Bassett, Virginia, in the early 1980s because of a girl that this book is dedicated. I came back due to my love of history. My connection to the town has been the best of times and the worst of times. In December 2014, I returned to this project after laying it aside for several years. During this time, I fought and beat cancer and saw the Bassett Historical Center leave the Blue Ridge Regional Library, a move I wholeheartedly endorsed.

One morning recently while waiting for the doors of the library to open, I found myself standing in the parking lot beside the Smith River when a train with four engines went by headed north on the "Pumpkin Vine" headed to Roanoke. I was struck by all the history that I was observing at that moment from the river that William Byrd crossed while he and others surveyed the state line between North Carolina and Virginia almost three hundred years ago to the train that sent Bassett Furniture all over the world from this small community in northwest Henry County, Virginia. It is always enjoyable for me to imagine all the people and events that come by standing at one point on any given day.

For the readers of this book if you find mistakes, I encourage you to contact me at freestateofpatrick@yahoo.com and tell me where I got it wrong. Constructive criticism is always welcome.

As thirteen colonies declared their independence from Great Britain, a movement was underway to form Henry County, Virginia, from its neighbor to the east, Pittsylvania County. In January 1777, Virginia formed Henry County. Named for the first non-British Governor of Virginia, Patrick Henry, who lived in the county from 1779 until 1784. A decade later, land from Henry County became Patrick County allowing map-readers to forever remember the name of the man who stated, "As for me Give Me Liberty or Give Me Death!"

Located along the border with North Carolina first surveyed by William Byrd in 1728, the county was home to the famous antebellum Hairston family. In the 20th century, textiles, furniture, and the chemical manufacturer, DuPont, made up the large industrial base of the county. With the recent outsourcing of jobs, the county is turning to other economic sources such as tourism as the Bassett Historical Center, which provided many of the photos in this book.

History is a strong part of life in the county. The land that is today Henry County was once Charles City County, a quarter century after the founding of Jamestown. Native peoples roamed this land long before the English first arrived in Virginia. Evidence of their life abounds in Henry County, researched in the last century by Richard Gravely and continued today by the Virginia Museum of Natural History located in Martinsville. The county is known as a place to research genealogy as the Bassett Historical Center is known worldwide and by this author as the "Best Little Library in Virginia." People come from all fifty states and overseas to research the collection house there.

Henry County was once part of Prince George and Brunswick Counties and later part of Lunenburg, Halifax and Pittsylvania County before the American Revolution, George Washington visited Fort Trial near the Smith River, which flows into the Dan River. The Dan River meanders back and forth across the state line until eventually reaching Albemarle Sound in North Carolina. The land of Henry County is comprised of flat piedmont and rolling hills. The foothills suffered from terrible floods until the Philpott Reservoir tamed the Smith River creating recreational activities for boating, swimming and fishing. Many of the photos in this book document the flooding especially the deluge of 1937.

During the antebellum period, Henry County was a place of tobacco and large plantations such as the one owned by the Martins, who gave the name to the county seat, Martinsville. The Hairston family dominated the landscape of the county that tradition holds you could walk across the entire length of the county east to west without ever leaving their land. The family owned homes in Virginia, North Carolina and Mississippi. Evidence of the Hairstons still exist in the county as some of their plantation homes still stand such as Beaver Creek and Marrowbone or in community names such as Magna Vista and Chatmoss. Thoughts of romance entered the mind of a young visitor to Henry County in the 1850s when James Ewell Brown "Jeb" Stuart courted young Elizabeth "Bettie" Hairston in 1852 and two years later at Beaver Creek north of Martinsville. Tradition holds she rebuffed the future Civil War General and later married her cousin J. T. W. "Watt" Hairston literally keeping the money in the family. You can still see the grandeur of their lives built on the back of slave labor. Today, the name Hairston is composed predominantly of African descent taking the name of their former owners.

Henry County contributed to the Southern effort in the War Between the States with many men. Only one significant visit by Union forces commanded by William Jackson Palmer, a brigade commander under George Stoneman, in one of the war's last raids in April 1865. Palmer, a Quaker from Delaware, grew up in Philadelphia and was a railroad man before the war. R. E. Lee surrendered at Appomattox Court House, on the day Palmer left Martinsville on April 9, 1865, after fighting Confederate Cavalry under the command of Colonel James T. Wheeler the previous day.

Railroads and industry dominated Henry County in the twentieth century. The Danville and Western Railway "The Dick and Willie," ran east to west through the county before terminating in Patrick County. The Norfolk and Western Railway, now the Norfolk Southern, came from Winston-Salem, North Carolina, on the way to Roanoke, Virginia, north of the county. Henry County became a crossroads of steel tracks that brought people and industry to and through the area.

The furniture industry centered in the county made Bassett, Stanley, American, and Hooker Furniture household names. Companies such as Bassett-Walker, Fieldcrest, Tultex, and Pannill named for the family of J. E. B. Stuart's uncle, William Letcher Pannill, made the county a hub for textiles in the twentieth century. DuPont came to Martinsville producing fibers that changed the world along the banks of the Smith River. Sadly, almost all this industry has left, forcing the county to rethink its direction.

Today, tourism via racing, history, and recreation from the Philpott Reservoir make up a large part of the county's economic impact. The Philpott Dam built along the Smith River created the largest manmade lake east of the Mississippi River. Piedmont Arts nearby offers a vibrant cultural setting along with the New College Institute and Patrick Henry Community College providing educational opportunities for a population in the process of change.

This book reflects this history focusing on the northwest section of the county from the Patrick County border to Highway 220 on the east. The images presented in this book are about half from the collection of the Bassett Historical Center, which will benefit from the proceeds of the sale of this book donated by this author along with the Greater Bassett Area Cooperative. Most of the images in this work came from people who brought their photos to the library for this author to scan. Those who shared their photos and memories drive the scope of the book. While many people and events will not make the images presented here, it is more important to this author to preserve the history of those willing to share and the library that will preserve it for future generations. Please visit my website www.freestateofpatrick.com to learn more about the history surrounding our county.

Contributors who assisted with this book and/or contributed photos and text to this book include:

Elva Adams
John Bing
Cindy Bingman
Joel Cannaday
Nancy H. Carnupp
Galilee Clark
Posie Collins
Teddy Compton
Anne Copeland
Matt and Ruby Davis
Andy Doss
David O. Dyer
Rebecca Dyer
Sam Eanes
Carolyn Eggleston
Joan and Jesse Frith
Ross Gale
Jennifer Gregory
Debbie Hall
Cindy Headen
Kenney Kirkman
Rachel Koontz
Jane Joyce Sharpe and Lynne Joyce Leonard
Jo Anne Philpott
Peter Ramsey
Craig Rockwell
Pat and Paul Ross
Betty Scott
LaVonne R. Smith
Fran Snead
C. M. Stafford
Douglas Stegall
Clifford Stone
Avis and Elbert Turner
Juanita Wells
Betsy Whitlow
Bill Young
Laura and Coy Young
and from the collection of the Bassett Historical Center

Chapter One
Elva's Chapter

Above, Employees of Bassett Furniture circa 1902. Below, Axton natives, David Eanes, Mike Westmoreland and Lee Gilley, are pictured here trout fishing in the Smith River at Bassett.

"Terry Martin was truly born under a musical star and he was a joy to watch and hear. He graduated from Fieldale High School in 1959 where, from the beginning, he had stood out as a really talented musician. He received a Master of Fine Arts degree in Music Composition from UNC-G, and he did graduate studies in music composition and orchestration at Boston University. He composed symphonies, band works, musicals, and popular music media. He served as Band Director at Bassett High School, John Marshall High School, Northern Nash High School, George Wythe High School for the Arts and All Souls Presbyterian Church. He was choir director at Fieldale Baptist Church, a pianist for bands, clubs, and country clubs such as the Burt Massengale Orchestra and the Woody Pittman Orchestra. At the time of his death on January 23, 2005, he was head of the music department at George Wythe High School for the Arts in Richmond, VA. He was interred at Greenwood Memorial Gardens in Goochland County, VA and is survived by his wife Lannie Beasley Martin. His musical creations are available on his original website at http://www.mmmm-music.com."

"Percy James Adams was born April 25, 1906, in Rockingham County, North Carolina, to George W. and Flora J. Adams. He married Willie Pearl Walker November 19, 1932, and they lived in Fieldale at 81 Field Avenue most of their married life. They had one daughter, Billie Dare Huff, and one granddaughter, Christy Landon. In his early years, he worked as a long-range truck driver for 13 years prior to the war. He drove for Bassett Furniture Co., Blue Ridge Trucking Co. and R. P. Thomas. He worked as an auto mechanic for 25 years, during which time he served one year as a Civil Service mechanic to the Army, stationed in Greensboro during World War II. He always loved car racing and building modified racers. During the time he owned and operated the Shell Service Station & Garage in Fieldale, he built two racers, #8 and #X-100. Although he never drove either car, he raced them at the Horsepasture Speedway and other small dirt tracks during the late 40s and early to mid 1950s. In 1956, he went to work as a Henry County Special Police Officer in Stanleytown, employed by Stanley Furniture Co. and Henry County. He was an officer for 15 years before retiring in 1971. He died July 20, 1984."

Local Orthodontist David Jones (second from the left) with Wayne Kirkpatrick of the Dan River Basin Association, (third from the left) I this group released baby brown trout into the Smith River behind the Bassett Historical Center in 2006. Henry County School Students, shown below raised the fish.

Letitia Ann Davis Hurd, grandmother of Anne Copeland at the Bassett Historical Center, is also the mother of Tilman Hurd, who operated an electrical supply store in Martinsville. Below, the gavel of the Patrick Henry Chapter of the National Society of the Daughters of the American Revolution on display at the Bassett Historical Center was made of leather wood from Patrick Henry's farm in Henry County.

Future teacher, coach, and historian, Larry Turner receives the Most Valuable Player Award at Bassett High School in 1963 presented by Dennis Hall. Below, Linda Dillard was the director of FAHI (Fayette Area Historical Initiative) until a traffic accident left her disabled. She is pictured here at the Bassett Heritage Festival in 2008. The FAHI, an African American Museum, is located in Martinsville, Virginia.

In 1970, *The Case of the Crushed Petunias* by Tennessee Williams was the subject of a one-act play by Bassett High School students at the Piedmont District Festival in February and at the State Festival in Charlottesville in March. The director was Linda Padgett. The student director was Lysa Hill on the far left with cast members Carol Anthony, Kurtis Teel, Pat Lipford, Larry Moran, and Karen Teel. Below, Quoth The Raven 'Nevermore" as Bassett natives Debbie Hall and Betty Scott look on at Tom Perry's program on Edgar Allan Poe, which was part of The Big Read in 2010 at the Bassett Train Station.

Melanie Daniel Turner and Anne Copeland in the new addition of the Bassett Historical Center during construction in 2010.

"She was born Betty Davis in Bassett. She graduated from Bassett High School in 1956 and Longwood College a few years later. She has a daughter named Dawn. In 2010, she is like the Ever Ready Bunny…she keeps on running. And running and running ... to tirelessly volunteer. I only know part of her life and it involves books. She is an officer in the Friends of the Library: treasurer now and formerly president. She is also treasurer of the Henry County Heritage book committee. And she is the current Chairman of the Board at the Bassett Historical Center. And goodness knows there is likely more. She is very capable and absolutely selfless. And she will make you laugh...most important! www.myhenrycounty.com named her Volunteer of the Year in 2010."

Shown below, the construction of the addition to the Bassett Historical Center. "The Bassett Historical Center has been called 'the best little library in Virginia'. From 1992 through 2004, their patron count increased 1359% over a period of 13 years. Since 1998, they have had an increase of 125% per year. People from all 50 states and 15 foreign countries have visited the Center. An expansion plan for the facility became reality in 2010. The addition added 4195 square feet to the existing building."

"Sometimes I am lucky enough to visit Susan, the web person, at Pocahontas Bassett Baptist Church. I say lucky because while we are working I can listen to Peter Ramsey playing the organ. On a real lucky day, he will play "In the Sweet By And By" for me. Right by my parking place is this Time Capsule. The best version of "In The Sweet By And By" that I've ever heard is by Dolly Parton in the CD album entitled 'Little Sparrow'."

From www.myhenrycounty.com "Who says history is boring? Not these two. They are John Redd Smith, III and John Redd Smith, Jr. visiting the Bassett Historical Center in Bassett on the first day issue of the Henry County Heritage Book. John Redd Smith, III is the grandson of J. Frank Wilson who is most fondly remembered by residents of Fieldale, Virginia. Below, on any giving day during season you will find people fishing in the Smith River behind the Bassett Historical Center. You will also find Canadian Geese and Blue Heron hanging around.

Betty Jo Brown Fulcher moderated multiple discussions of The Big Read in 2010 featuring Edgar Allan Poe. Here she is at the Bassett Branch Library. Below, is Tom Perry's presentation at the Bassett Train Station at Halloween on the real history of Poe.

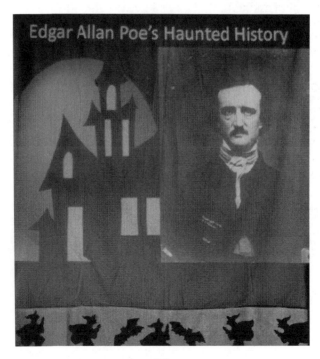

"The Bassett Train station is typical of many in its construction and its history. Once a busy Norfolk & Western stop it is better used than many today as it serves as a meeting place for various community events. On Thursdays during the warm months, it is something of a Farmer's Market. During the Bassett Heritage Festival, it houses displays of historical memorabilia. The local garden club keeps it decorated for the season as you can see here."

The First Bassett Furniture Plant known as "Old Town."

Chapter Two
Bassett Furniture Company

Bassett Furniture Industries celebrated its 100th Birthday in 2002 with a company picnic that included the families of the employees. Food, fellowship, games for the children, music, and fireworks were held in a fair atmosphere at the Jack Dalton Park in Henry County.

And the story of Bassett Furniture begins...it was 1902, in the foothills of the Blue Ridge Mountains of Virginia, brothers John D., Charles, and Samuel Bassett and brother-in-law Reed Stone formed the Bassett Furniture Company. Their total assets were $27,500. The period that followed was spent using innovation to create new furniture designs, to increase production, shipping, and sales, and to add factories and warehouses to the company holdings. The goal later became to make the name Bassett Furniture a household marketplace name.

From 1902 to 1912, the United States had only 76 million people inhabiting its 45 states. There were only 8,000 registered cars and fewer than 150 miles of paved highways. Coffee sold for $0.15 a pound. The average worker earned $0.22 an hour. It was the glorious age of Florenz Ziegfeld, Barnum and Bailey, The Great Pierce Arrow, and the Flying Machines. Tin Pan Alley was churning out these lilting tunes: A Bird in a Gilded Cage, School Days, and Meet Me in St. Louis. It was a happy time – a time of prosperity and progress. J. D. Bassett, Sr. had been traveling to Jamestown, New York, and Grand Rapids, Michigan, selling his fine Appalachian oak lumber to the industrious furniture companies. He became convinced he could do equally well in the manufacture of furniture. In 1902, the Bassett Furniture Company was formed to produce competitively priced bedroom furniture to meet popular tastes. At the start, the work crew consisted of about 50 inexperienced mountain men. Some of the men walked eight miles to and from work because of poor roads and lack of transportation to earn a five cents an hour wage. The first Bassett bedroom was a simple design in sturdy oak. With an abundance of oak virtually in Bassett's backyard, raw materials were easily obtained. Bassett was able to turn out furniture that was affordably priced. Large dressers sold for $4.75 while washstands were $2.75 and chifferobes were $4.00. Company records show the original sale of a bed at a phenomenal $1.50. Bassett workers were strong, rugged mountain men familiar with saws and planes and eager to work. Top furniture designers and salesmen were recruited. War and unrest had little effect on Bassett's continued progress. The prosperous years were marred only by a fire that completely demolished the factory. This setback was temporary. Out of the ashes rose a new brick plant, possibly the first motorized plant in the southeast, and a million-dollar company was ready for the post-war boom that was sweeping the country.

The Jazz Age – 1922 – 1932. Operations continued to expand with the formation of the J. D. Bassett Manufacturing Company to make bedroom and other types of household furniture. However, in 1925, fire struck again. Once more, out of the disaster, rose a rebuilt portion of J. D. Bassett Manufacturing for the production of dining room furniture. In 1927, the management purchased an unsteady Craig Furniture Company in Martinsville, renamed it W. M. Bassett Furniture Company, and turned it into a profitable enterprise. New furniture competitors were born from past Bassett associates, beginning the southern dominance in the furniture industry. Three Bassett furniture companies, each with its own sales force, actively competed with each other. J. D. Bassett called a "house divided" meeting, and in 1930 Bassett Furniture Industries, Inc., an umbrella combination of all three companies, was born.

The Period of Recovery – 1932 – 1942 were the lean years. The stock market crash plunged the country into Depression. On March 4, 1933, the banking system collapsed. One quarter of the labor force was unemployed. It was ironic that Bassett began a period of expansion at the start of this devastating depression. A new plant was constructed in 1930 to make chairs to match the design and the finishes of the Bassett suites. In 1934, Ramsey Furniture Company was purchased at public auction and renamed Bassett Superior Lines. Through careful management, Bassett survived the Great Depression with a solid financial structure. In 1940, the capital stock of Bassett Furniture Industries increased from $1,875,350 to $4 million. But war clouds loomed on the horizon. It was clear that furniture buying would soon halt for the war's duration, and Bassett began searching for ways in which to participate in the war effort.

The War Years – 1942 – 1952. At the onset of the war years, the Bassett corporate structure was solid and management was eager to hold the company together until the conflict was over. Soon after the acquisition of a substantial contract from Yellow Cab and Coach Company, Bassett Furniture Industries converted from furniture manufacture to the production of truck bodies for the armed forces. Its massive production facilities remained intact. With the end of the war came the huge housing developments all over the nation. With the new homes came demands for furniture to fill them. To prepare for this upsurge of business, Bassett wisely invested $6 million in modernization, and at the close of the decade, the renovated plants were turning out increased production. Bassett's already eminent position in the furniture industry was assured.

The Suburban Era – 1952 – 1962. The war marriages and the baby boom resulted in a pilgrimage to suburbia. They moved by the millions: houses went up overnight. Bassett bloomed with suburbia's demand for furniture. Floor space had doubled. New power plants and huge conveyor systems had been installed. Production peaked. At age 50, Bassett Furniture Industries employed 3,100 men and women.

The boom in housing brought changes in home furnishings. Quick to recognize the new trend, Bassett Chair Company was soon manufacturing a full line of living room tables, and in 1957, the Bassett Table Company was established.

Bassett, the town, became a company town and in 1961 had 3,500 residents, 500 houses (owned and rented to employees) a First National Bank of Bassett, Bassett Post Office, and Bassett High School. Bassett generated its own electricity from the early 20th Century, as was the standard practice for rural factories. The company sold furniture across the U. S., Canada, and the Caribbean Area with more than 150 salesmen.

The Age of Aquarius – 1962 – 1972. Acquisitions, building, expansions, and additions of new lines moved at a phenomenal pace. In 1963, Bassett built a new five –story warehouse and acquired Prestige Furniture Corporation for the production of upholstered furniture. Within just three months at the beginning of 1972, the first shipment of Day Dreamer reclining chairs was on its way to the dealers. The acquisition of E. B. Malone Bedding Corporation and National Furniture Company of Mt. Airy, North Carolina, had been included, making a total of 31 Bassett plants. Among the expansion projects of this period were the completion of the showroom building in Thomasville, North Carolina, a five story warehouse, a fiberboard plant in Bassett, the purchase of Art Furniture Manufacturing Company and the Taylorcraft Furniture Company in Hiddenite, North Carolina.

The Computer Age – 1972 – 1982. Bassett constructed and remodeled new facilities as well as purchased new plants during the 1970s. In 1974, Bassett acquired a case goods plant in Dublin, Georgia, and a juvenile products plant in Hickory, North Carolina. A new plant was completed in Surry County, North Carolina, in 1975 to produce the National/Mt. Airy line. In 1976, additions were made to the Dublin plant and the fiberboard plant in Bassett. In 1979, Bassett acquired the Weiman Company in Christiansburg, Virginia, to make and market very stylish (Heirloom) furniture for department stores, and fine furniture stores, as well as decorators.

The High Tech Era – 1982 – 1992. Bassett continued in its role as one of the world's foremost furniture makers, being named to the illustrious Fortune 500 as the 1980s came to a close. In August 1984,

Bassett purchased Impact Furniture located in Hickory, North Carolina. Impact manufactured popular priced occasional and bedroom furniture in three plants in the Hickory area. During 1984 Bassett implemented a Gallery Program to aid dealers in presenting furniture to the consumer, as it would actually appear in their homes.

Bassett continued its nationwide advertising on television and in major magazines and became one of the most recognized participants on such hit game shows as Wheel of Fortune, Jeopardy, and Let's Make a Deal.

Dedicated to Greater Progress -- 1992 – 1997. Bassett moved to the forefront of contemporary furniture design by building in Catawba County, North Carolina the first 100% polyester finishing facility in the United States, which used state of the art high gloss polyester finishes on furniture. The 200th Bassett Furniture Gallery was opened. The "furniture as you see it in your home," gallery concept, was well received by consumers who found furniture buying decisions made easier. Advertising in nationwide Women's and Home Magazines increased Bassett's brand awareness. Expansion of the Motion Division and updating equipment kept the company among the industry's most successful and respected companies. The purchase of a new Microsoft based computer system coordinated the management of manufacturing plant inventories, shipping, sales, and accounting aspects of business. Bassett introduced its own retail stores – Bassett Furniture Direct.

The Age of Innovation and Transition 1997 – 2001. In 1999, Bassett opened a plant in the Patriot Centre at Beaver Creek Industrial Park that focused on dining room tables. The entire process was engineered and designed to provide an environment for the employees that was not only unique to Bassett, but also unique to the industry. Process flow and ergonomics were two of the major advantages incorporated into the overall design. Through major advances in coatings technology as well as the equipment used to apply them, Bassett was able to introduce the "Indurance" finish.

Bassett moved its product showroom from Thomasville to High Point, North Carolina. In 2001, the company unveiled its new 80,000 square-foot showroom located in the International Home Furnishings Center. The showroom features prototypes of the company's Bassett Furniture Direct store and at Home with Bassett gallery. The showroom also boasts a full retail training facility, including a computer classroom and an auditorium. Bassett renewed its focus by dedicating efforts on its core business – wood and upholstered furniture marketed under its "Bassett" brand name. This focus allowed Bassett to better respond to the changing market place by producing more stylish products, to improve quality furniture by focusing on fewer product lines, and to better serve consumers with faster delivery times. Bassett focused to serve the consumer by providing three channels of distribution: its own retail stores, Bassett Furniture Direct; its in-store boutiques called "@Home With Bassett"; and through traditional channels of distribution such as J. C. Penney stores. These channels of distribution brought Bassett branded furniture to a broad range of consumers who appreciate high quality home furnishings at affordable prices.

Bassett announced in February 1990 that it would close its oldest plant, "BFC" built on the first original plant site. The 400 workers were transferred to other facilities in Martinsville and Bassett. In 1997, the W. M. Bassett plant in Martinsville was closed and sold to Martinsville City. May 2000 began a recession for the furniture industry. Product lines were re-evaluated according to sales and industry competition. Bassett began more importing of furniture for distribution and re-sale to complement its wood and upholstery furniture production. In September 2000, they announced that operations at J. D. Bassett and Bassett Chair plants were being consolidated, as well as operations at the Bassett Table Company plant in Bassett with the new dining room table plant #11 in the Patriot Centre. The company reviewed its operations for ways to become more efficient and bring operation cost, in line with business. In the year 2001, the year began with the bankruptcy of two of its largest customers, Heilig-Myers and Montgomery Ward and Company. In August 2001, Bassett announced that Bassett Chair Plant and rough mill operations would be closed. The company was increasing imports of occasional tables and cribs and reducing production of wood products. J. D. Bassett and the Bassett Chair plants were closed. The year 2001 will be remembered as the year of big manufacturing downsizings.

A Time of Restructuring, Realignment of wood manufacturing operations, Retooling, and focus on Customizable Furniture Products 2001 - 2010. The economic downturn that first affected the textile industry hard in Henry County with Tultex, Vanity Fair at Bassett, and other plant closings, now was having its effects on the U. S. Furniture Industry. Reasons like the increased importing of furniture from other countries; sales of self-assembled wood products sold at large retailers; and the slowdown of the new housing market started the decline of furniture production in Henry County. Superior Lines was changed from a production facility to an assembly and warehouse facility. Shipping operations were given to Zenith Transport. The National /Mt. Airy division was closed and its facility was made into a Bassett Furniture wood production facility, and then later closed and became a warehouse location. Other plants and locations outside Henry County have also been changed to reflect the economic conditions of 2008 and 2009. Henry County was now experiencing 10 – 11% unemployment in all areas of the job market as the 2008 over-stated housing market had a down turn and the U. S. began bank bailouts and loans to the car industry and made other economic changes.

A look to the future. Bassett has become more consumer driven. It now relies on sales of customizable furniture and other products where one table and chair design is offered in different finishes or one upholstered chair or sofa frame is offered in many fabrics, and design variations. They are producing items one at a time, according to the consumer's order, by focusing on products that can be customized, produced, and shipped faster to the consumer than ever before. And it all began with a vision. – Cindy Bingman

John D. Bassett, Sr.

Above, salesmen of Bassett Furniture meeting in Chicago, Illinois, January 1931. Below, the original Bassett Furniture Company.

Below, the continued expansion of the company in the 1950s with the addition to the Bassett Chair Company.

Described as a group of "Old Timers," many generations worked for Bassett Furniture over the many decades.

Bassett Furniture dominated the town of Bassett above in this photo and below American Furniture, plant dominated this photo of Martinsville.

Making furniture at Bassett included the Machine Room where glued pieces of wood were held together to dry.

(Left) Interior view of the Machine Room.
(Right) The Cabinet Room, reflecting the ideal working conditions prevalent in every department of this plant.

Below, the Riverside Hotel on Main Street in Bassett.

Above, the letterhead from Ramsey Furniture.

Delivering furniture from Bassett involved not only the railroad, but also many times trucks took over the streets of the town to deliver furniture. Below, locomotive switching cars at North Bassett.

Above, trucks loaded with furniture in front of Nathan's Department Store. Below, John D. Bassett, Sr. on the far right with trains that carried his furniture. His son, W. M. Bassett is third from the left.

Bassett Furniture spawned other furniture companies such as Stanley above and Hooker below.

Above, Bassett Furniture salesmen meeting in Chicago in 1953.
Below, an early view of Bassett including Bassett Furniture Company.

This view shows the Bassett Furniture Company office on the far right beside the original furniture plant. Notice the company homes and the proximity to the Smith River, which before the Philpott Dam would wreak havoc on the town.

This view of South Bassett shows the Bassett Superior Lines with Highland Street in the foreground including the Jarrett and Adams homes in the center. To the right of Superior is Valley Veneer with the first W and B Chevrolet on the far right. P. M. Ingram and Son is across from Superior Lines.

The rear of the present Bassett Furniture Industries offices with the swinging bridge over the Smith River that was destroyed by a flood in the 1970s and was not rebuilt.

Bassett Superior Plant, Bassett, Virginia

Bassett Printing Company

Built by Bassett Furniture Company of mahogany from the African Congo for Curtis Brothers Furniture, the "World's Largest Chair" sat at 2041 Nichols Avenue in Washington D. C. Weighing 4,600 pounds, the chair was nineteen feet high, nine feet wide, and twelve feet deep. It represented the furniture industry, which was a vital part of the economy of Henry County.

"Home of the World's Largest Chair"

The chair, in the foreground of Curtis Bros. Furniture Co., built of solid Africa mahogany stands 19½ ft.—weighing 4,600 lbs. It was built in Bassett, Virginia by the Bassett Furniture Industries—the world's largest manufacturers of wood furniture.

PLACE STAMP HERE

CURTIS BROS. FURNITURE CO., NICHOLS AVE. AT V ST., S.E.
WASHINGTON 20, D. C.

Fishing in the Florida Keys during the 1920s are John D. Bassett, Sr. with wife, Pocahontas, and Charles C. Bassett with wife, Roxie. The Hundley sisters married the Bassett brothers. The brothers along with Reed L. Stone started Bassett Furniture Company, which today has over 130 stores in North America.

Repairing the building's brick facing and cleaning windows while a police officer and people watch along the Reed Stone Block in Bassett after World War II. Stone, with the Bassett brothers, started the furniture company to the left of the Reed Stone Block.

Helen Mildred Bassett in Rome, Italy, in the 1950s. She lived in Texas, but traveled the world. The daughter of Samuel Henry and Eliza Joyce Bassett came back to Bassett for her final resting place. Her father along with his brothers, John D., and Charles C., and brother-in-law, Reed L. Stone, began Bassett Furniture Industries.

The W. M. Bassett Furniture Company of Martinsville in the early 1900s, probably after 1930. William M. Bassett expanded the family's furniture factories to nearby Martinsville by purchasing Craig Furniture in 1927. The son of John D. Bassett, Sr. became unhappy with his position within the family company and branched out on his own. On the next page above is the home of John D. and Pocahontas Bassett, the latter sitting on a trunk with maids, Mary Hunter and Gracie Wade, to the right. Above, John D. Bassett, Sr. with chauffeur, Pete Wade fishing at Hobe Sound, Florida.

Above, Queen Elizabeth II with Bassett son-in-law and Virginia Governor, Thomas Stanley, in 1957 along with Prince Phillip, Hugh Chatham, Stan, Crockett, Rob Chatham and Anne Pocahontas Bassett Stanley. Below, Bassett Furniture Company Offices was located to the right of "Old Town."

Above, Hooker Furniture Company in Martinsville. Below, Thurston Manor, home of Mr. and Mrs. C. C. Bassett.

Chapter Three
Bassett Folks

In this photo, contrasting the changes in transportation with the coming of the automobile versus the farm wagon, is Mary Druscilla "Grandma Sissie" Bassett Ramsey (1862-1950). The wife of John W. Ramsey and the daughter of John Henry and Nancy Jane Spencer Bassett was doing her "daily chores" including feeding chickens.

Mary Druscilla Bassett Ramsey with her three daughters Mary Wootsie R. Giles, Lucy Belle R. Joyce, and Nannie Laura R. Helms circa 1915. With the world just a few years away from world war and the coming of the industrial revolution in the form of furniture and textiles, this image reflects a more bucolic time in Henry County.

The first doctor to practice in Bassett beginning in 1908 was Dr. Charles M. Ross shown here with his family.

Above, Dr. E. N. Shockley served the Bassett community.

Dr. B. F. Noland was the second doctor to practice in the community in the building later occupied by Turner's Shoe Shop. Mrs. Effie Hunter Noland, the wife of Dr. Noland started the first library in Bassett in the upstairs above Dee's Drugstore. Below, Dr. L. A. Faudree also practiced medicine in Bassett from 1946 until 1984.

This author appreciates the efforts of Dr. John P. Bing shown outside his Bassett office in 1969. He worked tirelessly collecting photos for this book. He called, cajoled, and brought photos to the Bassett Historical Center to give this author over 1,700 images from which to choose the photos represented in this book.

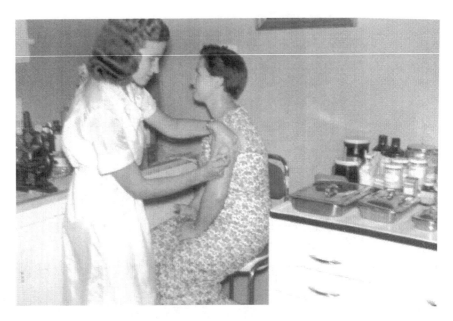

Registered Nurse Marie Haynes Ashworth shown in 1959 giving a shot to a patient in the office of Dr. John P. Bing. The office, located in front of the Bassett Furniture Headquarters, was the site of Bing's practice for twenty years beginning in 1955. Marie worked there for one year. Below, Miss Virginia 1958 Barbara Guthrie Kelly with Dr. Bing in 2012

Below, Jay Paul Bing, age ten riding Bourbon in the Figsboro Horse Show in 1967.

Joan P., Jo Dee and Dr. John Bing

Dee Dee Bing Hennis, the daughter of Dr. John P. Bing and his wife, Joan, on "Sassy Maid" in a 1963 North Carolina State Amateur Championship. Married to Dan Hennis, she lives near her late parents' home in Bassett. She has two children and three step-children, two grandchildren and five step-grandchildren.

Paul Ross acting as manager for Ace Frehley of KISS aka Jennifer Gregory at a Halloween program on Edgar Allan Poe at the Bassett Train Station operated by the Greater Bassett Area Cooperative.

Educator John Bruce Harris was the first African-American principal in Henry County at Campbell Court Elementary School. Harris worked tirelessly to preserve the Black History of the area. Today his work continues with efforts of the Fayette Area Historical Initiative. Compared often with the work O. E. Pilson, both of their collections are housed in the Bassett Historical Center.

With twenty-five years' experience in law enforcement, Benjamin A. Smith was Captain and Investigator of Bassett Police. The first African-American to hold such a high position in Henry County law enforcement, he later worked as Chief of Security for Bassett Furniture Industries. Married to Lois Pilson, the couple had three daughters.

Either enticing visitors to an auction or having fun afterwards Leila Grogan, Jessie Herman, Shine Jones, Codell Jones, Marie Grogan, and Virginia Belle Franklin literally poke their heads through the sign directing visitors to a land auction. Marie married Charles Eugene "Gene" Clay, and they are the parents of Patricia Ross, Director of the Bassett Historical Center.

The cover girl for this book sitting in a sandbox on Third Street in the northern part of Bassett where the factory now rests along the Smith River is Avis Ellen Carter Turner, the daughter of Clifford and Ida Hollandsworth Carter and wife of Elbert Turner. Avis donated many great photos for this book as she did for my previously published books.

On October 22, 1902, the entire town of Bassett including the American Legion Post No. 11 Junior Drum and Bugle Corps came out to celebrate Bassett Industries. They held the celebration on the baseball field of the Bi-State Baseball League, which is still a baseball field today behind the Bassett Public Library located across the street from the Bassett Historical Center. Bassett Furniture expanded into J. D. Bassett Manufacturing, Bassett Mirror Company, and Bassett Chair Company. They acquired Craig Furniture in Martinsville making it W. M. Bassett Furniture and Ramsey Furniture making it Bassett Superior Lines. Sons-in-law of the Bassett Family, Thomas Stanley and J. Clyde Hooker, formed Stanley and Hooker Furniture Companies, which are both still viable businesses today. Another son-in-law, Taylor Vaughan, and his brother started Vaughan Furniture. In 1938, a public stock offering raised over 2 million dollars giving Bassett Industries more reason to celebrate.

P. M. "Doc" Ingram, Clenard Ingram, and Harold Stone at the 1939-40 New York World's Fair. P. M. ran a grocery store in the south part of Bassett. Stone owned two grocery stores, one north and one south in the town. At the fair, the three Virginians got a look at the "World of Tomorrow" and the world of the immediate future as World War II began during the fair.

In 1943, Patricia Clay Ross and her collie dog "Wiggles" were favorites of her uncles Terry Frank Grogan Jr. and Carl Melvin Grogan. The young men were the children of T. F. Grogan and wife, Trudie. They were home during their service in World War II in this image. Pat, the daughter of their sister, Marie, is now director of the Bassett Historical Center.

Virginia Belle Franklin Farmer, Codell Jones Wade, Marie Grogan Clay, and Jessie Williams Herman hitchhiking and showing a little leg in knee length hose to entice a ride along a dirt road near Bassett Virginia. It is often a shock to think of parents as once being young and goofing around with friends.

This image of Albert Frank Thomason and his wife, Cassie Metz Thomason, comes from circa 1930. They lived in the Bassett Forks area of Henry County. Their seven boys and five girls were Harold, Wilson, Beatrice, Dillard on the first row. The second row includes O. C., Madoline, Ramey, Thelma, Glenwood, George, Celesta, and Simmons.

These students from the National Business College of Roanoke are in the lobby of Bassett's Riverside Hotel in the 1930s. Standing are Horace N. Wright, Nellie Haney, Ellen P. Gale, and Luther Baker. Sitting are Wilda Coleman and Agnes Park. The furniture industry created a need for trained young people to work.

One of the first Henry County baseball teams was from Bassett in 1929. Among those identified are W. T. Carter, Howard Holbrook, Smiley Bullock, Trixie Bryant, Early Woody, Jubal Mitchell, George McCraw, Melvin Grogan and Bill Beam. The county produced many professional players such as the Detroit Tigers Lou Whitaker.

Andrew Miller, son of Johnny and Linda Miller of Bassett, played at Bassett High School before matriculating to Virginia Tech, where he was a mainstay on the offensive line of the Hokies until graduating in 2013.

Father and son catchers, Randy and Todd Hundley have a Bassett connection. Randy Hundley grew up in Bassett, graduated in 1960 from J. D. Bassett High School before playing Major League Baseball for five teams, but mainly for the Chicago Cubs. His son, Todd shown below also played for the Cubs and was famous for hitting home runs on opening day.

The Bi-State League was consisted of minor league baseball teams from Virginia and North Carolina, The Bassett Furnituremakers played in it from 1935 until 1940 at Riverside Park. The team made the playoffs ever year and won the championship from 1936 through 1938. Managed by Ernie Jenkins, Ray White and Walter Novak, the team was affiliated with the New York Yankees, Cincinnati Reds and Brooklyn Dodgers. The Furnituremakers played teams from Mount Airy, Reidsville, Fieldale, Martinsville, Danville, and others in the two states. Many baseball players came through Bassett playing for the Bi-State League. A few made it all the way to the Major Leagues and the Baseball Hall of Fame. Among them was Enos Slaughter, who played for several teams among them the St. Louis Cardinals and the New York Yankees, where he was on four World Series Champions.

Phil Rizzuto "The Scooter" played in Bassett in the Bi-State League. He went on to a Hall of Fame career with the New York Yankees playing shortstop. He was a seven time World Series Champion.

Shirley Jean Davis circa 1952 in the Miss Tobacco contest.

Livie and Parks Davis in the summer of 1952 at Lover's Leap.

Betty and Shirley Jean Davis hanging around on their father's bumper.

Chapter Four
Smith River

One of three swinging bridges, which were the main mode for pedestrians to cross over the Smith River in Bassett. This bridge contains a strict warning to those brave enough to venture out over the waters of the stream first named Irwin, then Smith. In the watershed of the Dan River, both rivers begin their journey to Albemarle Sound in North Carolina in neighboring Patrick County, Virginia.

The swinging bridge over the Smith River behind the world headquarters of Bassett Furniture was a popular place for children and adults to fish just downstream from the Bassett Historical Center. Today these bridges are gone, but the center preserves the history of these bridges through the preservation of these images. Below, "Canadians" even visit the Smith River behind the Bassett Historical Center.

The flooding Smith River wreaked havoc on the town of Bassett many times over the years until the Philpott Reservoir was built. This 1940s carnival, warned of the impending flood, did not take it seriously until it was too late to move to higher ground. Today, the Philpott Dam controls the Smith River flow with daily releases of water.

The original Bassett High School shown in the right of this image was not immune to the flooding Smith River. Notice the woman under an umbrella and men sitting on top of railroad cars while inspecting the rising waters of the river before the Philpott Dam regulated its flow.

This image of the flooding Smith River shows the company houses of Bassett Industries at the location today of the Bassett Historical Center.

This 1940s image of the flooding Smith River in Bassett, Virginia, shows the tower of the First Baptist Church on the right and Lee Telephone Company, now Century Link on the left. As a note of geography, the riverbed is several hundred yards to the right of the railroad tracks shown covered in water. Below, south end of the Stone Block in the 1940s including Stafford's Jewelry, Cab Stand, Gulf Station and Prillaman's Oldsmobile.

Bassett comes from an application for a post office dated 23 March 1892 and named for the John Henry Bassett family. Sawmilling temporarily stopped in the village the year before furniture making came on the scene. The community was once the largest manufacturer of wood furniture. There is a document signed by President Franklin D. Roosevelt and Postmaster General James A. Farley declaring Mrs. Rosa L. Williams as Postmaster of Bassett in June of 1939. So, we know that the S was still part of the name of Bassett in 1939. There are also a Bassett, Nebraska and a Bassett, England.

Above, the Bassett Post Office built in 1938, shown during a 1940s flood.

Below, Bassett High School during flood was torn down in 1948. Today, it is the site of the former office of Bassett Furniture Company.

Below, you can see the steeple of the First Baptist Church to the right of the lone railroad car.

Above, the Bassett Train Station during one of the 1930s flood.

One of the worst floods along the Smith River was in 1937. This view of downtown Bassett looks south and east at Mitchell Motor Company. It is unclear whether the Standard Oil and Gas created an environmental hazard due to the flood, but the rising water eventually led to the building of a dam.

Floodwaters from the Smith River engulfed the Riverside Hotel in downtown Bassett in 1937 in this image from a postcard. In spite of the constant flooding of the town, the industrial growth of the furniture industry after the Great Depression and the coming world war continued to allow the community to rise again.

Charlie Elgin's diner, Texaco filling station, and the Lee Telephone Company, now Century Link in the 1937 flood of the Smith River. Today only the telephone building remains. Notice the loading platform for the railroad. The waters cover the tracks. The riverbed was behind the white house to the far right to give the reader an idea of how far the river left its banks.

This image of the flooding Smith River in the northern section of Bassett shows the furniture plant with the houses shown in the foreground. Bassett was a company town of the Bassett Furniture Industries and many of these "Company Houses" still remain today along Route 57, the Fairy Stone Park Highway, up and down the street on both sides of the Bassett Historical Center.

One of the many floods along the Smith River destroyed this swinging bridge in Bassett. Today, the bridges are gone reflecting the loss of history that the Bassett Historical Center tries to preserve. Bassett Furniture's headquarters and two warehouses still stand in the town, but the heydays of the industrial boom from one hundred years ago are gone.

During the 1940s flood, Bassett town jeweler, C. M. Stafford, is shown on the left with Maynard Lackey is third from the left.

"This photo is a little different from most of the old flood shots. It shows Main Street in Bassett, VA looking toward the river and includes the old Bassett High School. This photo is of a Bassett High School, which stood where Bassett Furniture's Corporate Office Building is now. On the left is just an edge of a Norfolk and Western boxcar. Boxcars do not change much in appearance over time. And at the right are some stores. Bassett is glad to have Philpott Reservoir in place upstream. Although the Fieldale stretch of the Smith sometimes rises over its banks Bassett is spared."

Mrs. R. L. Hutcherson in 1975 at age 80 still crossed the swinging bridge over the Smith River as a shortcut to her bank.

Below, the bridge in 1972 with Bassett Furniture offices in the background.

Today, the Smith River is a place for recreation with the Henry County Parks and Recreation Smith River Trails system.

Chapter Five
Train, Train

Bassett Furniture Company began as two sawmills providing cross ties to the Norfolk and Western Railroad. With the coming of the train, the family began the furniture business when Charles, John, and Samuel Bassett along with brother-in-law, Reed L. Stone, came together in 1902. The result shown in this photo is a boomtown with factories belching smoke into the sky and commerce proceeding below.

The growth of the furniture industry and the coming of the railroad in 1892 made Bassett grow from the inception of Bassett Furniture Company in 1902. The train station built for loading cargo still stands today and is the focal point of history during the annual Bassett Heritage Festival each September.

A winter view of the downtown Bassett train station in 1969. Trains still come through daily headed for Winston-Salem, North Carolina, from Roanoke, Virginia, but sadly, stops in Bassett are just a part of history due to the loss of the furniture industry locally. The station opens now for the yearly Bassett Heritage Festival and the summer Farmer's Market sponsored by the Greater Bassett Cooperative. Across the street is Trent Furniture Company and the Riverside Hotel. The flooding Smith River dominates the Bassett Train Station covering the tracks in the downtown area in the 1940s. These tracks used by the Norfolk and Western, now the Norfolk Southern, are still in use today mainly carrying coal for the Duke Power Plant in North Carolina.

Above, the Norfolk and Western K class engine with a passenger cars. Below, a north bound N and W freight train in Bassett.

Virginia Ore and Lumber Company, better known as the Fayerdale Railroad, at what is now Fairy Stone State Park. Below, the Norfolk and Western Depot at Bassett was replaced by the brick depot in 1922. Fire destroyed the wooden structure.

The rear of a southbound coal train rolling through Bassett in 1976 on the Norfolk and Western, now Norfolk Southern Railway, shows what once was and will never be again. A caboose, seldom seen anymore, makes up the rear of the train as it passes through traveling between Roanoke, Virginia, and Winston-Salem, North Carolina.

Norfolk and Western trains meet north of Bassett at Philpott, Virginia, on June 20, 1974. Diesel engine GP-9 #789 is northbound to Roanoke, Virginia, on the left, and southbound is First 53 SD-35 #1554 headed for Winston-Salem, North Carolina, on the right. Below, northbound Norfolk Southern steam train excursion coming through Bassett in 2012.

A Train excursion came through Bassett on June 24, 2012. It was a restored Southern Engine 630 coming from Winston-Salem, North Carolina, to Roanoke, Virginia. People placed pennies on the track for the train to make a memento of the event.

Jennifer Doss and son Hunter, a Thomas the Train fan wait for the steam train to come on June 24, 2012.

Above, Norfolk and Western steam train switching cars at Bassett Furniture circa 1942.

Chapter Six
School Days

Trey Harris is the Director of Bands at Bassett High School. Under his leadership since 1996, "The Bassett High School marching band, winter guard, and indoor percussion ensembles have been successful participants at local, regional, circuit, state, and national competitions. They have many regional class championships and finalists accolades with Bands of America as well as being a nine time Grand National Semi-Finalist. The Marching Band program is the current seven time Class 5 Open USBands State Champions. The band has also finished in the top five in their class at National Championships for the last 5 years. The winter guard and indoor percussion ensembles are proud members of the Atlantic Indoor Association Circuit. Last year the winter guard earned the bronze medal in A1 and the indoor percussion earned the silver medal in PSA at Circuit Championships. Both groups have consistently been WGI regional finalists and World Semi-finalists." You can read more about the band at www.bassettband.org.

Bassett High School opened in 1978 replacing the John D. Bassett High School, now owned by EMI. The varsity football team won the AA Region IV championship in 2006. Prior to consolidation with Fieldale-Collinsville High School, the school won the state AA girls' basketball championship in 2000 and the AA boys' track title in 1980. A Golf Championship was won by boys in 1970 and boys basketball in 1959.

Bassett High School 1920-48

     The first high school in Bassett was an old one-room log building located on the land of a Mr. Price at the corner of Bassett Heights Road and Pine Valley Drive. The exact date of the founding of this school is not known, but it was prior to 1900. The building had slabs that were used as seats with holes bored near the ends and pegs inserted for legs. Poorly lighted, the building was heated by an open fireplace at one end of the building.

     This school was later abandoned for a school located nearer Bassett when the Bassett sawmill was beginning to attract residents to the community. This school was located on the property of John Henry Bassett near the John D. Bassett Park. The two-room frame structure was built and donated by the community. Some of the teachers who taught in this school were Joe Ramsey, Etta Burse, and a Miss Wade.

     With Bassett Furniture Company being founded and built, the community saw a large increase in population. Thus, a larger school was needed and again John Henry Bassett donated another site. A building was built adjacent to the Riverview Primitive Baptist Church near the homes of Mr. and Mrs. Reed L. Stone and Mr. and Mrs. J.D. Bassett, Sr. This building was a four-room frame structure, which was enlarged by the addition of another room in 1909, the same year that the first secondary school classes were offered. With a five-teacher faculty, two years of high school were added to the current curriculum. Emma

Carter, Nannie Mitchell, Mr. Barnes, and Mr. Coe were the persons serving as principals of this school during the period 1909-1915.

This five-room building continued in use until January 1915 when the school moved to the completed brick structure in town. This building, costing approximately $30,000, was built jointly by the district school board with the citizens of the community. The old school building was sold at public auction December 6, 1916 and the money was applied to the cost of the new building.

A third year of high school was added during the session of 1916-1917. At that time, the school still employed five teachers: three full-time grade teachers, one full-time high school teacher, and one teacher who divided her time between grade and high school.

The year of 1923-1924 was the first for the school to be accredited by the State Department of Education with a full four-year course to be offered. Miss Crickenberger was the principal.

"River Ripples" was the school's first newspaper, published in 1925. Ten years later, "Timber Tints" was published, the school's first annual. The school supported sports, football especially, with a good Bassett team. During this time, there was no mascot, so a contest was held to name a mascot for the school. Charles Eugene "Gene" Clay, a 1932 graduate of Bassett High School, coined the school's nickname, the Bassett Bengals. Through changes over the years, the mascot for the school remains the same, the Bengal.

In 1937, the enrollment in this school increased from 358 to 785, which made further expansion a necessity. A new unit was built at a cost of $60,000.

During the War years, 1941-1945, many activities had to be curtailed. Interscholastic sports were practically abandoned due to the rationing of gasoline for travel and a scarcity of equipment. Difficulty was also experienced in finding and keeping enough teachers for the classes in operation. After the War, things began to get back to normal and the school reorganized the sports program. Football was a major sport, along with basketball and baseball.

In 1947, a contract was signed for the construction of a much needed modern high school building at the cost of $750,000. This was more than double the $300,000 that had been appropriated for the same work in 1941. So, in the fall of 1948, the school session opened in the new and modern high school building, which had been built to accommodate five hundred students, a hundred less than the six hundred maximum capacity. At that time, the school was officially named John D. Bassett High School by action of the Henry County School Board. Also during this session, a new department, Diversified Occupations, was added. This provided both class and "on the job" training experience for those students who did not expect to go to college. John D. Bassett High School met education challenges under the leadership of four principals: E. Carl Hoover, A. F. Waleski, G. E. Nolley, and Lewis W. Morgan.

Classroom additions became necessary during the early 1960s, and plans were again made for the construction of a new high school for Bassett students and students in other areas of the county. In January 1975, construction began on the new 185,000 square-foot Bassett High School on a 78-acre site with a target date of completion in May 1978. August 24, 1978, marked the opening day for the new school, built by John W. Daniels and Company of Danville, Virginia.

The school was being partially financed with $2 million in bonds issued through the Public School Authority of Virginia and loans of $750,000 from the State Literary Loan Fund. Plans included a football stadium, other athletic fields, two 1,000 space parking levels, and a chain link fence that would surround the 78-acre site.

With a watchful eye on the construction, Henry County School Superintendent Dr. Paul H. Jones said the new gym would seat 3200, as compared to 375 at the J. D. Bassett High School.

Enrollment for the school would be at least 975, with the transfer of students from G.W. Carver High School and Fieldale-Collinsville High School. Maximum capacity for the new school was 960. Almost one fourth of the county's high school students would attend Bassett High School.

The J. D. Bassett High School was not closed when students moved to the new high school. It was reopened as Henry County's first middle school. Current sixth and seventh graders from Sanville, Mary Hunter, Campbell Court, and Stanleytown Elementary Schools transferred to the old JDBH. This reorganization of elementary grades put kindergarten through fifth grades in elementary; sixth, seventh and eighth grades in middle school, and ninth through twelfth grades in high school.

When J.D. Bassett Middle School closed, it was sold to E.M.I. Imaging, Inc. of Stuart for use as their main offices. David Wright, a 1960 graduate of J.D. Bassett High School, purchased the school from Henry County, and he and his family have certainly taken care of the "old" school. The gym has never looked better, the lockers are used for storage units and the home economics department has been used as a "home away from home" for the Wrights on nights when they have worked late. Framed photographs of the senior classes from 1948 to 1978 line the hallways. The library has been turned into a conference Room. The chemistry and biology labs are still there with desks, books, and a mannequin that looks like one of the teachers. The cafeteria has all new equipment and class reunions, as well as a luncheon for Governor Tim Kaine, have been held there. The auditorium, where, believe it or not, students were allowed to watch the World Series, has been used for history symposiums sponsored by the Bassett Historical Center as well as other community events. John D. Bassett High School/E.M.I. Imaging, Inc. was listed on the National Register of Historic Places in 2006.

Reed Creek School students beginning with front row (left to right) First row: May Stone, Jasper Wagner, Frances Dyer, Virginia Mullins, Billy Young, Hester Morrison, Frank Carter, Betty Ann Davis. Second row: Randolph Brown, Mitchell, Maynard Buckner, William Blankenship, Claude Cobler, T. B. Cobler, Junior Hodges, Jessie Cahill, Frank Still, Harry Kirks, Jimmie Still. Third row: Billy Hodges, Keever Mullins, Leon McMillan, Douglas Koger, Sloan, Martha Cobler, Mary Stone, Helen Carter, Coleman, Francis Koger. Fourth row: Clarice Brooks, David Dyer, Josephine Koger, Clemons Morrison, Pauline Brooks, Coleman, Eunice Davis, Douglas Davis, Virginia Young, and Myrtle Bowles (teacher). Fifth row: Elsie Thomason, Leslie Lackey, Junior McMillan, Edward Wike, Lewis Cobler, Clyde Cahill, A. J. Mullins, Cecil Lackey, Una Mae McMillan.

The Reed Creek School was located north of Bassett Forks on the west side of Rt. 220 at the present location of Crouch's Nursery. This photo shows the wonderful Myrtle Bowles in the mid to late 1930s when she taught grades 1 to 5. The school was made of brick and had a wooden folding door used at times to separate the students into two classes. The windows were tall and provided light as there was no electricity. The teacher opened the windows with a mechanism on the end of a pole during warm weather for air circulation. Outside the school, there was a hand pump for water and an outhouse as a restroom. Students would pump the water into a bucket and bring it back into the schoolhouse. Students used a metal dipper for drinking from the bucket when thirsty. Inside the school had a potbellied stove used for heat in wintertime and for cooking soup to supplement bag lunches brought by the students. Jay Foster Hollyfield was Superintendent of Henry County Schools at the time of this photo.

Students came from many neighborhoods including Rough and Ready Mountain Road now known as Melrose Road, Oak Level Road, and Bassett Forks. The students walked to school from their homes, as there was no bus transportation with the furthest students walking about two miles. All the students knew each other fairly well from being together in class for several years. They sat at desks with inkwells built into the top. Miss Bowles used a blackboard and books to teach reading, spelling, writing, arithmetic, history, and geography. Students played softball, hopscotch, tag, "annie over," and "ring around the roses" on the lot south of the school during recess. -- David O. Dyer

Campbell Court Elementary School

Another structure in Bassett on the National Register of Historic Places is the John D. Bassett, Sr. High School built in 1946-47. It received this designation in 2006. The school ended educational use in 2004, is now owned by EMI, and is the sight of many community events.

<u>Historic John D. Bassett High School</u>

Through these portals, many of its graduates have become true leaders in both our past and present society. Teachers, CEOs, artists, professors, congressmen, inventors, writers, tradesmen, governmental leaders local, state, and national, as well as nationally famous ball players, you name it and you will find that many students coming out of the John D. Bassett High School have been blest to have made the grade. Apparently, God saw fit to place the necessary teachers, principals, industry, and natural resources here in the Bassett area that has enhanced the gifts of learning to those that have been blest to live, teach, and go to school here. Whenever one tours the halls here and observing the pictures of those that have attended on the walls, you will always hear someone exclaiming how a person pictured here, or there, has distinguished themselves in their service to GOD, our nation, as well as our society as a whole, in virtually every walk of life to date except the President of the United States. Who knows, but what that position is yet to be filled!

The Historic John D. Bassett High School is now registered as a Virginia Historic Landmark, as well as on the National Register of Historic Places by the United States Department of the Interior in 2006, by the David E. Wright Family (a 1960 graduate and a son of Robert Lee Wright 1901-1994)

The school was constructed in 1947 – 1948 in the town of Bassett in Henry County, Virginia and officially opened in the fall of 1948 with the first graduating class being 1949. It is an excellent example of a two – story Georgian-Revival style school built after World War II, the last school to be constructed in the state of Virginia with an ornate exterior, thus marking the end of an era of school design in Virginia. (The 1954 school-planning manual issued by the Virginia Board of Education stated, "no funds should be expended for extraneous ornamentation unless every desirable education facility has been provided in the buildings".

The John D. Bassett School has three – bay entrances which provides public access to the two community spaces in the interior – the Auditorium at one end, and the Gymnasium at the other. The center corridor on the first floor connects with the front and rear corridors to form a "B" for Bassett, when seen from the air. The spaces of the "B" also create two courtyards for an outside atmosphere.

The original school has been kept or restored where possible to its original condition including the science lab, library, and home economics. The home economics with its accompany suite of rooms is 2,800 square feet, representing one of the largest home economics departments in the state.

In 1961, additional classrooms were added to the back of the school, bringing the total square footage to 85,000. The school continued to serve as a high school until 1979 when it was converted to a middle school. Due to consolidation of schools in Henry County, Bassett Middle School closed permanently in 2004 and the property was sold to EMI Imaging in January 2005.

The Historic John D. Bassett High School is owned and operated by the David E Wright Family and is now a multi-purpose facility. EMI uses a portion of this building (one of four), to securely house and retrieve original, microfilm, and digital information for government, business, and medical facilities, in addition to the corporate offices for EMI Imaging, EMI Recycle, and EMI Security.

By 2014, the school has included a Visitor Welcome Center with a "Consignment & What Not Shop", as well as a place for all types of Community Social Functions, including Seniors "Game On"- a place for seniors and their guest to enjoy all types of activities, Training Centers, and group tours, There are also spaces available for rent including; a 585 seat Auditorium, a Dining Hall with accompanying outside decks for seating for up to 300, a Gymnasium, a Library for up to 125, and various classrooms that can be used for crafts with seating for 30 to 50 people, or as possible incubators for other businesses. –David Wright

"Doug Joyce snapped this photo in the Fieldale gym about 1961. The Fieldale players are #22/Bug Purcell, #13/Gator Hundley, #21/Floyd Bryant, #24/Billy Prillaman, and #12/Eddie Gibson. Around the court edge are some familiar faces. Just behind the basket is B.J. "Big" Carter. To his left is his wife Margaret Carter. Continuing on clockwise are Coy Campbell and Mrs. Campbell, Jean Fuller (leaning for the shot I think), Maxine Thomas, Marie Knight, Mary Robertson and Mr. Robertson, Wayne Eanes, Delo Dove Eanes, Floyd Bryant, Judy Joyce Bryant, ?, ?, Rose Rakes, ?, Jo Ann Hancock. Peeking out from the door behind Margaret Carter is school Principal Ronald Iler. Next to him is Bassett Principal Al Waleski. And seated just under the backboard is Steve Daniels or possibly his brother. The man two seats to Steve's left may be Jimmy Paris. The Bassett players are: #33 Jackie Cooper, #35 James Carter; #35 Frankie Moore; #25 Andy Hayes; #22 Paul Hatcher; #43 Jim Joyce."

"Back in 1961 Fieldale High played home games in the Community Center gym. As you can see here, the overhanging balcony was packed. These players in white are all members of the class of 1961. #22 is Bug Purcell. At far left is Gator Hundley. Hidden near the center is Eddie Gibson. At far right is Billy Prillaman. Jumping for the tip is Barney (B.J.) Carter. There are two things you may notice right away in this picture that are very different from today. 1. Nowhere in the whole picture is there an ounce of fat on anyone. 2. Those boys wore some really nice short pants. Thank K.C. for this wonderful picture. Photo by Doug Joyce. Bassett Players are #33 Jackie Cooper; #35 Frankie Moore; #25 Andy Hayes; #22 Paul Hatcher; #43 Jim Joyce; #23 James Carter; #43 is Sammy Collins."

"This play, a Moliere comedy, was produced by the Dramatics Club at John D. Bassett High School on November 21 and 22, 1969 in the school auditorium. It was Bassett teacher Linda Padgett Hollandsworth's first high school production. Cast members from left to right are Ben Craig (English 10), Johnny Martin, Lysa Hill (English 10), Suzette Gourley, Bahns Stanley, Carol Anthony, Linda Plogger, Larry Moran, Karen Teel, Pat Lipford, Frankie Philpott, and Mike Fizer. Photography by John Pankovich." Below, "Here's a group of actors from 1983. They made up the cast of a play at Bassett High School and were directed by Linda Padgett Hollandsworth. 1st row (l to r): Renee Coates, unknown, Carol Boyd, Joyce Boyd, George Ingram. 2nd row (l to r): unknown, Sharon Craig, Terrilan Wade, Corin Ortlam, Mark Stidham, Ruby Dillon, Steve Southerland (maybe?), Tonya Martin. back row middle may be Scott Stoneman"

This cute Tom Thumb wedding took place in Bassett, VA approximately 60 years ago. Tom Thumb Weddings and Maypole Dances seem to have gone out of style.

"Children pictured here at Walter Bondurant's fifth birthday party in Bassett, VA are: back row left to right: Andy Hayes, Katie Yale, Ann Snead, Mary Ann Lipford, Frances Lee Arendall, Barbara Joyce, Peggy Clark, Edward Barnes, Bob Hollandsworth, Dickie Williams, Hugh Chatham and Jimmy Joyce; Middle row left to right: Judy Pankovich, Betsy Stone, Harriett Bassett, Susan Roberts, John McGhee, Carol Philpott, Martha Jane Wells, Kathryn Austin, Butch Jarrett, Diane Young, Pat Clay, Stan Chatham; Front row left to right: Bucky Williams, Wesley Wells, Walter Bondurant, Fran Lipford, Sammy Collins. The photo is from December of 1947."

Ethel Marie Nunn and Betty Davis, head majorette, in the 1956 John D. Bassett High School Band.

John Ellyson Ramsey was Drum Major in the 1955 John D. Bassett High School Band.

Donnie Doss #35 playing for John D. Bassett High School against Drewry Mason in the 1960s.

The 1934 girls' basketball team of John D. Bassett High School. The young women were Margaret Holbrook, Cynthia Nolen, Galilee Smith Clark, Georgia Philpott Ingram, Marie Grogan Clay, Shine Jones Grogan, Ellery White Adams, Clovis Nolen, and Nellie Philpott Newman. In 2000, the successor Bassett High School won the girls state championship in basketball.

The John D. Bassett High School Drum and Bugle Corps in a parade possibly in Roanoke, Virginia. Today, the Bassett High School Bengal Band follows in the footsteps of those shown in this image. The new high school opened in 1978 and the older became a middle school. Two years later the high school won the boys state track championship. Below, the 1959 Virginia State Champions were 19-4 included Wendell Young, Jimmy Eanes, Eddie Stone, Wallace Hill, Bobby Quesinberry, Buck Gale, Herman Dodson, Clyde Stone, Calvert Fulcher, Jim Blessing, Edward Barnes, Randy Hundley, Mike Hall and Ace Prater.

The fifth grade class at Bassett High School in 1929. First row: Mrs. Charlie Waney, Mrs. Melvin Grogan, Mrs. Don Calaman, Billy Johnson, C. M. Stafford, unknown woman, Cletus Turner and Mrs. Roy Beamer. Second row: Frank Ingram, unknown woman, Robert LeFeaver, Mrs. Albert Clark, A. L. Philpott, John Helms, Mrs. Frank Ingram, and Mrs. Albert Williams. Third row: Mildred Ramsey, Ruby Southard, Johnny Ausborne, May Plybon, Virginia Crews, and S. K. McCall.

The Bassett High School Class of 1926 reflects the "roaring twenties" in their clothing. The front row left to right are Frances R. Frick, Dorothy B. Rich, Leslie Craig, Janie Turner, Sallie Jarrett. In the center are Mary Lindsey and Alma Coleman. The back row includes John Young, unknown woman, Bernard Craig, Julia J. Hickman, and Chester Helms.

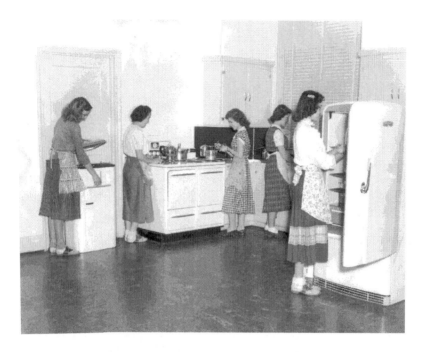

Home Economics Class at John D. Bassett High School include Shirley Hundley and Ann Stone

Majorettes including Kathy Ashworth, Kim Bryson, Denise Hall, and Debra Turney in the 1970s.

Below, Coach Bruce Lemon's girls team.

Bassett High School Cheerleaders. First row: Emily Ruth Messer and Stuart McGhee. Second row: Rebecca Adams Ellis Stone, Mary Campbell Craig, Bobby Webb, and Rhonda Weinstein. Third row: Tom Martin, Otis Amos, Peggy Philpott, and Lucy Lee Brammer.

Football Queen Betty Jane Jones and King Yancey in 1949 at John D. Bassett High School. The court includes Mary Swain, Nancy Helms, Yancey Arendall and John Philpott.

Above, John D. Bassett High School, now EMI. Below, the old Bassett High School.

Below, 1962 Bassett Football Team practice with Johnny Snead, Andy Cundiff, Billy Koger, Stafford McKenzie and Butch Barnes.

Heather Miller with Coach Patrinda Toney after Miller scored her 1,000th point for Bassett High School in 1998.

Chapter Seven
Around Bassett

Above, Mitchell Motors was located where Bassett Funeral Home now stands. Below, Dan Rodgers, Jubal Mitchell and Raymond Stone at the 1939 showing of new models.

The Reed Stone Block.

Above, Stanleytown building contained post office, grocery store, and doctor's office. Below, organized in 1898, Bassett Memorial Methodist Church stands across the one lane bridge that included a pedestrian walkway along with the homes of M. F. Mason on the right and E. P. Craig on present day Riverside Drive on the left.

Above, left to right: Fletcher Smith, Sue Collins and D. B. Robertson.

Middle photo is the old Bassett High School with fence added after 1922. Below, North Bassett furniture plants.

Below, Russell's Drive In with Tina Brown on the left and Shelby Brown, daughters of the owner.

Above, Blue Ridge Hardware retail store.

Above, the second W and B Chevrolet. Below, Bassett Oil Company with owner Lynwood Craig on the right.

Above, Bassett Mercantile Company was located across from the present day train station.

Top, Stanley Furniture Company. Above, Chocolate Bottom company houses with Bassett Chair Company and J. D. Bassett Plant.

Above, Bassett Superior Lines. Below, Ramsey Furniture.

Above, North Bassett Theater, the J. D. Bassett Plant Office and Wood Mercantile. After the theater closed, the building became Stone Mercantile. Below, the second location for the Bassett Public Library, over Kroger store. It later moved to old Bassett Elementary School after fire damage.

Above, on corner where Carter Bank and Trust now sits along with Peter Craig home and Craig Funeral Home. Below, Missionary Baptist Church, the first church in Bassett.

Above, Rough and Ready Mill. Below, the view of town from Bassett Heights area.

Above, Gunsler home on the left with Prillaman Oldsmobile on the right, taken from C. C. Bassett's home. Below, one of the earliest pictures of downtown Bassett.

Above, Bassett Table Company with Bassett Superior Lines in background. Below, Bassett Mirror Company.

The Bassett Post Office has a "Fresco" painted in 1938 by Walter Carnelli (1905-1959, native of Austria) as a project of the Treasury Department, Arts Division, started by Franklin Roosevelt during the Great Depression. The images painted on the wall depict the furniture making process.

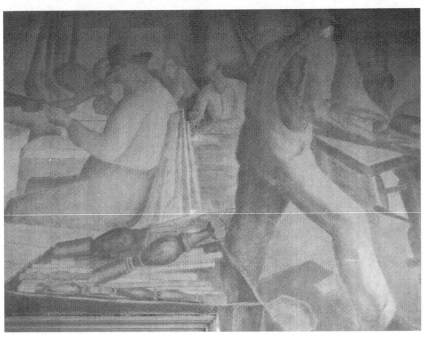

"President Roosevelt was inspired to take 500,000 young men off the streets and welfare rolls and give them jobs at $30 month. His program was called the Civilian Conservation Corp or CCC. The young men worked at building dams, planting trees, building state parks, repairing roads and so on. They built Fairy Stone State Park in nearby Patrick County. Roanoke newspaper publisher Julius B. Fishburn donated the 4,868 acre site, making it the largest of the six original parks, and one of the largest to this day. The CCC provided the labor and materials for the construction of the park and worked from 1933 until the CCC camp was removed in the spring of 1941. Roads, trails, picnic areas, cabins, a restaurant, bathhouse, dam and sanitation system are all part of the original CCC construction. Their handiwork is still evident in the park's log cabins."

Bassett once had three movie theaters such as the one in the Stone Block shown above.

Thurston Manor, built in 1902 by C. C. Bassett, was the home of the J. E. Bassetts and still stands at the top of the stairs today.

Above, is the home of John D. Bassett, Sr. The Bassett brothers married the Hundley sisters. Below, before Exxon there was Esso, owned in south Bassett by C. E. Clay and C. Melvin Grogan and later by Peanut Plaster.

Stafford's Jewelers was first on the Stone Block. Below, the Bassett Bank Building, S. H. Hooker General Merchandise, and C. C. Bassett Furniture Company before 1910 and Undertaker with the Post Office.

Bassett Superior Lines was once Ramsey Furniture Company. The plant along with Bassett Table Company burned in March 2012. Below, Bassett Mirror Company was organized in 1923.

You cannot help noticing many of the company houses still standing in town like these in North Bassett, which were tore down to build the Bassett Fiberboard Plant. Below, Norfolk and Western engine rolls through Bassett in the 1960s.

Started on the site of the W. M. Bassett home, the U. S. Post Office still stands in town. Before this building, the post office was in J. D. Bassett's merchandise store, C. C. Bassett's Furniture Company and Undertaker. Below, the homes of E. M. Hollandsworth and Curtis Bassett can be seen during one of the many floods of the Smith River.

Below, the Reed Stone Block had Dee's Drugs, Stafford Jewelers, Hundley Insurance, Elite Beauty Shop, Helms Shoe Shop, Sink's Barbershop, Hamblen Café, Wilkerson Café, pool hall, bowling alley, Western Union and Dr. Shockley's office upstairs. George Reynolds and his crew are painting the mortar.

Gone, but not forgotten, the first factory built in Bassett remembered as "Old Town" Below, Thurston Manor, the home of C. C. Bassett above Missionary Baptist Church with the home of Walter and Callie Scarborough Ramsey between.

The original Bassett High School built in 1915 was located beside the Riverside Hotel. Below, John D. Bassett High School built in 1948 became a middle school in 1978.

The Bassett Train Station above right and below was for the transportation of people, timber, and furniture for many years. Passenger service ended in 1961. Today the Bassett Community Market uses the structure every Tuesday and Thursday. The 1958 Ford drives past Trent Furniture Corporation, Village Soda Shop, Riverside Hotel and a theater. Below, boosters from Roanoke visit Bassett.

Chapter Eight
Hogue and Joyce Craig

Conversation with Hogue Craig is a walk through the history of the Bassett area. His description of buildings and their locations is vivid and his recollection of people gives you the feeling of their presence.

He was born December 11, 1921 to Della Davis Craig and Jesse Craig – their only child born in West Virginia, his family having a short brush with the coal mining industry before returning to Henry County. His grandfather was married three times and fathered large families with each wife; Hogue is a grandson of the third marriage.

He has brothers, Ciflo, Russell, Bill and Jimmy, and a sister Christine. All were talented in woodworking, as well as in music. Christine decided to become a beautician and opened a beauty shop in Bassett. She had at least one male customer, which was a little unusual in those days.

All of Hogue's brothers were in the military during World War II. Hogue was exempt because of a birth defect. Luckily, all of his brothers survived active military service.

Joyce Claypool, fresh out of Radford College, while she was teaching at John D. Bassett High School met Hogue on a blind date arranged by a mutual friend, Elwood Stone. They were a match! For the first ten years of their marriage, they lived in the Blackberry area, another area resplendent with Craig family history. They have two sons, Ben, born June 29, 1950 and Jim, born March 9, 1958. Joyce was raised by her grandmother – her mother was not very close. Yet when her stepfather died suddenly, Joyce responded immediately to the call in the middle of the night by driving to Pearisburg, Va. and bringing her mother home. Gladys became a member of the household and honored Joyce's "house rules." She was honored to be promised a burial plot in the Craig cemetery, and she remained a respected member of the family until her death eight years later.

For over 50 years, Hogue worked for Bassett Furniture Company, in the sanding room at "Old Town," his daytime job. He has long been well known and respected in the collectibles and antiques world. His pricing and selling knowledge, along with friend Cecil Trent, contributed greatly to the success of the Bassett Methodist Church's semi-annual yard sales. He cares for a vegetable garden behind their home. He is proficient at many things, a "handy man" and in addition has always encouraged young people to work for folks, whether as a volunteer or as a paid helper. Joyce retired from teaching in Henry County schools and frequently has former students approach her to tell of her influence on their lives. She continues to serve in many volunteer activities. Hogue credits Joyce with the happiness, contentment, and success of his life.

The Craig family owned over 200 acres in the area from present day Russell's Drive In and up the mountain. Pete Craig's home was built at the top of the hill. There is a Craig cemetery in that general area. Also Jesse, Hogue's father, attended a school in this area named New Hope School.

The property on which the First Baptist Church stood on Main Street, with the clock tower near the present site of Harder's Drug, was deeded to the church by the Craig family, Jesse Craig specifically. When plans were being completed for the Church to be relocated on the opposite side of the river, the pastor, Rev. White, discovered the deed transfer had never been recorded, so Jesse had a little fun pretending any document signed on Sunday was not legal.

Hogue and Joyce moved into Hogue's childhood home on Riverside Drive while Della was still the woman of the house. This home was a comfortable place not only to 3 generations of Craig, but also at times, to boarders. The house was built by Jesse and his brother Pete. They did not use a blueprint, but their own plan – rooms were large, equipped with closets, and conveniently, but some unconventionally located doorways for adult privacy and for overseeing the children's safety. The floors are hardwood; the woodwork retains its original finishes. Another plus is that the house was built on land high enough to escape the repeated flooding of the Smith River.

The large Jarrett farm was located near the Craig home. Mr. Ed Jarrett would drive his carriage to church, leaving the buggy in the stable practically next door to the Craig home while he attended the Methodist Church. Another family, the Burchfields, who helped establish Bassett Methodist Church, also lived on the same street.

The Methodist Church and the Craig house are a few doors apart. Long ago, the water used by the Church was from a spring behind the church where townspeople also stopped for a cool drink. Hogue recalls the job of cleaning the spring out, the last time with help from dentist, Dr Andy Lipford. This hillside has numerous springs, but the spring near the Church had been cemented and was used not only for the church, but by townspeople also it during lunchtime and after work.

For a time, the Craig home was one of a few in existence on Hundley Road (named for the Hundley Family, another landowner.) A 1923 map identified the road as Hunter Street but it was actually called Hundley Road. Hogue witnessed the road originally located near the river bank, then moved slightly away from the river into the pastureland – changed from a dirt one lane, to a gravel two-lane, then changed to a wider tar and gravel road and finally paved with asphalt. As a very small child he watched a man drive a wagon pulled by what he thought were cows. His father explained they were oxen. He saw Mrs. Molly Hopkins sitting proudly driving her horse and buggy. He saw a local matron enjoy her Packard auto. He saw a lady receive an automobile for selling the most subscriptions to the local newspaper, the Bassett Journal, a publicity plan of Mr. Scoggins, the owner of the paper.

Hogue witnessed the spectacle of many factory workers carrying lanterns as they walked over the hill in the early morning darkness from the Blackberry area toward one of the four swinging bridges to get to work in the furniture factories before daylight. Two of these townspeople were Joe Foley and Tom Taylor. Swinging bridges were conveniently located in North Bassett, Old Town, and Ramseytown, or South Bassett. The last remaining bridge was behind Bassett Furniture Industries corporate office and finally was not replaced.

Hogue talked with Pat Ross about the "Old 97," the old bus that traveled around town picking up workers to get them to work on time, bringing them home for lunch and again in the evening. Pat Ross recalled waiting for her "Papa" and her uncle to get off the bus. Hogue recalled the bus driver was Cline Conner.

The present site of the Bassett Historical Center is the location of the first permanent building for the Bassett Public Library, which opened to the public in 1955. Hogue recalls when Mr. Ed Bassett spoke of the need to build the library building and Mr. Nathan Weinstein offered to give $500.00. Hogue emulated Nathan's dialect which brought a flood of memories of Nathan –his department store, Nathan's, his fair treatment of his customers, his extending credit to some very young people and his generosity in helping young people by giving them part-time work during holidays and summers which not only helped the families financially, but it also helped the young people stay out of trouble. Nathan and wife Mollie's home is a few paces down the street from Hogue's home.

Hogue recalls prior to the new Trent Hill road being constructed, now Rt. 57N, there were many hog pens along the riverbank. When he describes it, you can almost hear the swine squealing, and you shudder to think of the "aroma" when the wind was blowing in your direction. This area is where the road begins the climb uphill just past the bridge near Poppa's Pizza.

Hogue remembered the streetcar café on the Stone Block. The streetcar was brought from Danville. He remembered the movie theater in North Bassett, which closed when the Stone Theater opened downtown. The young man whose job it was to transfer movies between the theater in North Bassett and the one downtown was probably happy when one of them closed.

Hogue gave the true reason the area in North Bassett was called Chocolate Bottom. It was because the first people to live in the company houses there were black people, not because of the dirt deposited by the flooding of the Smith River. He also gave us the location of Hell's Hollow - beside and behind the glass factory in North Bassett. He remembered Joycetown was named for Mr. George Joyce. Mr. Joyce married into the influential Ramsey family. His home was built on the corner across from R. M. Wright's Appliance Store now a part of Bassett Office Supply, and later belonged to Harold Stone and his family. It was decided the cluster of company homes built in this area were to be identified as being in Joycetown.

Hogue witnessed the arrival by train of the men working in the Civil Conservation Corps, who were then transported to their destination a few miles west of Bassett to begin building Fairy Stone State Park.

Hogue told of Bassett Furniture Company making the "practice" rifles for the military during World War II, as well as the wooden truck beds for the military transport trucks. His brother Bill recognized one of the Bassett-built truck beds while he was serving in the military in England.

Hogue remembers the first cab driver in town, Joe Cahill, a black man, who had no designated "stand," and the next cab owner, Verge Ferguson who would pick up fares getting off the train, and just for fun, drive the fare to North Bassett and circle back to their destination, the Riverside Hotel, just across the tracks from the station. Verge built the little "cab stand" beside Stafford's Jewelers. Mr. Roy Martin also had a cab service in North Bassett. There was also a cab service for a short time in Ramseytown.

Also, the first "service stations" were operated by such people as "Fats" Stanley and Ernest Hill. There was a service station in Ramseytown, between Ingram's Store and present day Buren Thomas's Used Car Sales, as well as "Shorty" Barnard's place which probably served more hot dogs than motor oil or gasoline. An old photo of the service station in the Stone Block shows an Esso sign. Some local automobile dealers were Jubal Mitchell who sold Packard cars, Ralph Mitchell, Prillaman Oldsmobile Co. and W & B Chevrolet, owned by Claude Woody and Mr. Belton. When Mr. Belton was no longer a partner, it remained W & B Chevrolet. In recent years, Jim Mills operated an automobile dealership in Bassett, and the G.R. Nelson family operates several dealerships. There is speculation that McGuire Philpott and Kermit Wray practiced speeding up the ramp at the side of the Oldsmobile dealership and stopping quickly before running off the high end of the ramp. There were also early Used Car businesses.

Hogue recalled Pedigo Davis operated the Mick or Mack grocery, and the Kroger store was operated by J. L. McGhee. Lelia Lipford spoke with "Whit" Sale about J. L. McGhee, and "Whit" hired "Mac" to become one of the personnel at Blue Ridge Hardware & Supply Co. and Virginia Machine Tool Co. Other grocery stores were Marsh's, owned and operated by Mr. & Mrs. Floyd Marsh, then owned and operated by their son, F. E. Marsh, Cooper and Ratcliff, Akers'(still in business), Saul's, Winn-Dixie, and most recently, Food Lion. P. M. Ingram's store was originally a wooden building, burned, but was rebuilt of brick. Valley Grocery also was wooden, burned, and was not rebuilt. Stone Mercantile had the same fate. It had been a three-story building. The two upper floors were rented rooms. The building also had porches on the front on the upper levels. Valley Grocery, owned and operated by Fred Plybon, also had rooms for rent on the upper floor, and some of the Ingram family lived in the upper floor of their store building.

Hogue also recalled laundry and dry cleaners from the old days – F. W. Mitchell owned one – his wife Marie taught piano lessons; also Rhodes Cleaners. Hogue is a member of the Knights of the Pythias. He recalled the days of the Pythias Hall over the Stone Block buildings. Local doctor Titus, was also well known in Bedford so much so that their Pythias building was named Titus Hall. Dr. Clifton Titus was relocated to Bedford during World War II by the government. Bassett had sufficient doctors according to population and Bedford did not. Hogue named other doctors who practiced here many years ago, such as Dr. Hunter Powell Nolen, Dr. Elmer N. Shockley, Dr. D. L. Fleischman, and Dr. Charles Ross. Two patients of Dr. Ross had been celebrating a little too much and informed Dr. Ross they felt so bad they just wanted to die. Dr. Ross agreed to help them. He lined them up against the wall, told them to put their hands up, and he pulled out a gun. [It was not loaded.] The two young men believed Dr. Ross might actually shoot them, so they began begging the doctor not to shoot. They decided they did not feel as badly as they had claimed. Dr. John Bing also settled here as a general physician. He was a well-known researcher and historian.

Hogue recalled the drug stores, Mountain Drug, Dee's Drug, and Harder's Drug. He also remembered the early funeral homes, Craig and Bassett, which originally, only sold caskets and the Pete Craig house on the corner across from Bassett Methodist Church, which at one time served as a funeral home. Also located in Bassett were Collins Funeral Service, now Collins-McKee, and Bassett Funeral Service.

Hogue remembers Wright's Appliance Store, Adams Furniture Store, Trent Furniture Store, Nolen and Stone Furniture, the Feed Store – the older one uptown – Swain's Seed Store in Ramseytown, James Wall's Appliance store, J. P. Daniel's store and Mike Quinn's store at

Oak Level. North Bassett stores included Stone Brothers, Ernest Stone had a store at North Bassett bridge, Wood's Store, the first "Red Pole" Stone store, later operated by young "Red Pole", and Norman Divers operated a service station/used car business/garage. There were rooms on the second floor of most of these buildings used for both businesses and living space. Pete Craig's early home was on the corner at the bridge on Hundley Road. A brick wall was built around it because so many vehicles ran into the house. This house was demolished when the road was improved. Currently Carter Bank is located close to the corner, although the Craig house was further away from the riverbank.

Hogue, his brothers, and their friends had some narrow escapes with automobiles careening around the curves on the Jarrett Hill section of Blackberry Road. These adventures have collaboration from other local gentlemen who were friends of Hogue and his family. Those curves were eliminated when the road was "improved" some years ago.

There have been declarations of appreciation from some of Hogue's contemporaries that he is the person who guided them through their youth to become responsible and dependable adults. Hogue, himself, credits his wife Joyce for influencing him from the first day he met her to live in an upstanding way and to behave in such a way that would be pleasing to her. They have both been long-standing members of the Methodist denomination. Hogue can talk with you about many businesses, people, and events that occurred in Bassett during the past 80 years. What a pleasure it is to sit with him and Joyce, whether to recall the "good old days," or to speak of current events. All of the things Hogue speaks about are from firsthand knowledge. He has an excellent memory, and his expressions make the events of yesterday come to life to be enjoyed again. However, that does not mean he lives in the past. He and Joyce have an intense interest in today's events and today's people Hogue's walk through the history of the Bassett area hand in hand with Joyce continues. – Betty Scott

Chapter Nine
Unknown Bassett

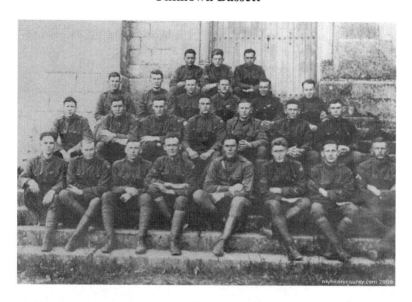

This photo from the Bassett Historical Center is one of many unknown images of people forgotten. The identify of only one soldier is known. One of the things the Center tries to do is identify those in the many photos in their collection. Send any ideas on identifications to baslib@hotmail.com. You can visit the center and look at the many photos that needed identification.

Chapter Ten
Blue Ridge Hardware and Supply Company

In the early years of his career, William Whidbee "Whit" Sale, an industrial supply company representative from Taylor-Parker Company, Norfolk, Virginia began calling on Bassett Furniture Company, quickly becoming friends with Ed and Doug Bassett. They encouraged him to start his own industrial supply business in Bassett. There was a good market in Henry County – furniture businesses and textile companies were opening and growing.

In 1929, Blue Ridge Hardware and Supply Company's doors opened. In addition to the "nuts and bolts" of industrial supplies, a division to manufacture and sharpen cutters opened in 1936 as Virginia Machine Tool Company. Five days after installing a new electric salt bath furnace in that division, the building, located behind the Stone Block, burned to the ground. A new building in "Ramseytown" beside the office/warehouse was built. This metal building became a storage area and a larger VMT building was built behind the main office/warehouse. This location was beside Valley Veneer Company. The Valley Veneer location is partly now a street connecting Rt. 57 and Rt. 57A, intersecting with Blackberry Road, and a warehouse for Bassett Furniture Company. Retail stores were opened in Bassett and in the Banner Warehouse in Martinsville. A fire in 1951 destroyed Banner Warehouse and all the businesses located there. Blue Ridge did not reopen in Martinsville. By the late 1970s, other branches opened in Lenoir, Burlington, North Carolina, and Christiansburg, Virginia. An Engineering department and a retail division opened in Bassett. These branches employed over 100 people. The Retail Store in Bassett was originally located in the present parking lot of Bassett Furniture Industries corporate office, relocated to the renovated Hub Department Store building where in 1970, this building suffered a fire.

As the economy began changing, textile businesses began leaving the area followed soon by furniture manufacturing. The out-of-town branches and the Retail Division closed. In 1992, the B.R.H and S was sold to owners in Big Rock, Virginia, becoming Blue Ridge Industrial Supply Company In 2002, the new owners closed the company due to more drastic economic decline. Virginia Machine Tool division was purchased locally and remains in business. The warehouse building was offered at auction Saturday, October 4, 2003. The contents were sold; however, the bid for the building was not certified. It was sold at a later date and now houses Light Electric Company.

BRH and S gave employment to many families, both in Virginia and North Carolina and in the 1970s became one of Virginia's largest industrial supply houses stocking over 90,000 items. Virginia Machine Tool Company was a Southern leader in the production of tools, cutters, etc. The success of this company resulted from the hometown honesty and integrity of the owner, and the recognition of the talent and capabilities of his employees. William W. "Whit" Sale was born in Norfolk, Virginia on March 23, 1903 to John Bowman Sale and Fannie Weaver Sale, one of 3 children. He graduated from Maury High School and attended Virginia Polytechnic Institute, Blacksburg, Virginia The 1910 Federal Census listed John B. Sale as a mill supply representative. (Must be in the genes.) "Whit" and Virginia married in 1928, moved to Bassett in 1929, and continued to make their home in Bassett until their deaths. Virginia was born on August 31, 1900, in Norfolk, Virginia to Walter Jackson Blalock, Sr. and Fannie Mangum Blalock, with two sisters, and one brother. Virginia quickly became a close friend of her next door neighbor. They decided to treat some lady friends to lunch. Virginia had no children and her friend had two by then, so they decided to serve lunch in her friend's home and do the cooking in Virginia's home. They did not want their guests to see them carrying the food across the yard, so they used a baby carriage to transport the food. The lunch was a big success and no one was the wiser of its delivery. "Whit" served on the Selective Service Board during WWII and was a member of Kiwanis Club, Elks Club, Masonic Order, Board member of First National Bank of Bassett, Memorial Hospital of Martinsville and Henry County, Chamber of Commerce, Blue Ridge Council BSA, Bassett Public Library, Welfare Board Charter member (1938), and Bassett Memorial U. M. C. Virginia was a 30 year volunteer for American Red Cross, and Bassett Garden Club. Both were avid supporters of Ferrum College partly because it began as a working farm and as a mission to educate regional students. They supported a scholarship fund established in their name at Ferrum College and assisted with the Performing Arts Center there. Virginia supported a local Ruritan Club. Both enjoyed tennis and golf; Virginia played golf into her 90s. She was also a member of Bassett Memorial United Methodist Church. "Whit" passed away Sunday, January 30, 1976, having been married to Virginia for 49 years. Virginia died Monday, January 26, 1998, at age 97. They left no children, but felt that education was mandatory for young people. Their influence is still felt in their generosity through Ferrum College and through the W.W. and Virginia Sale Foundation. – Betty Scott

Chapter Eleven
More Bassett Images

The Hotel Bassett.

Every September the Bassett Heritage Festival takes over the town on the second Saturday. The 2005 event is shown here. Below, the Bassett Rescue Squad is always ready to come to the aid of those in need.

Above, Bassett Printing Company. Below, A.D. "Dove" Nolen, circa 1935. Dove worked for Bassett Chair for many years, and later purchased a dump truck in order to sell scrap materials from the factory. Impressed by his work ethic, J. D. Bassett suggested he purchase a truck to do furniture deliveries around the state. Dove later went on to found the A.D. Nolen Trucking Company.

Dwight and Roxanne B. Dillon with Raymond Burr, famous for his television roles as *Perry Mason* and *Ironside*, the killer in Alfred Hitchcock's *Rear Window* and a memorable 1950s role reporting on *Godzilla, King of Monsters*. Below, another mid-1930s scene from Bassett Printing Company.

Above, Judy Turner Nolen, circa 1930. After her husband, Isaac Alexander Nolen, died, Judy moved to Bassett. On March 22, 1957, on her 100th birthday, Judy was honored as the oldest citizen of Henry County. Below, the father of seven children, Wilbert Stone and his wife, Laura, resided in Bassett for most of their lives. Wilbert worked for Bassett Furniture and eventually became the foreman for the Plant 1 Finishing Room. He was a charter member of Bassett Church of the Brethren, and later moved his membership to Mount Herman. He served as Treasurer for many decades at Mount Herman until his death in 1981.

Above, Jesse Frith. Below, Jesse Frith, Jim Thomason, Roy Byrd, and Ray Frith

The Frith Children: Ray, Jesse, Jack, and Nellie.

The Henry Thomas Williams with wife Rosa Lee Philpott, George "Red" Arthur Williams, Ruby Williams Bassett, Albert "Preacher" Williams and Christine Williams Jarrett.

Charles Bassett with his father, J. E. "Ed" Bassett, Sr.

Ed Bassett with sister Dorothy Bassett Rich.

Joseph Benjamin Bassett and his wife, Sallie Alma Coleman. Below, the Machine Room at Stanley Furniture in 1935.

Clarice Joyce Roberts   Lucy Ramsey Joyce
Harriet Hundley Ramsey   Mary Drucilla Basnett Ramsey

From right to left. Front row: Clyde Mitchell, Maynard Mason, George Franklin, Posey Ingram, and Fred Craig. Second row: Dewey Mabe, Edd Helms, Hamlin, Jim Stafford, and Elmer Shockley.

Spencer Morton drives Santa in his T-Model Ford in the Bassett Christmas Parade in 1964. Below, Paul Roberts continues the tradition in Young's Barber Service.

Leonard H. Wagoner at the Rough and Ready Mill circa 1920.

Homer Hairston operated Homer's Roller Snack Bar behind John D. Bassett High School in the mid-1950s and 1960s. While blind, Homer was known for his ability to know exactly how much change you gave him for Mallo Cups or PomPoms. Below, Evona and Laura Adkins with their aunt, Brenda Prillaman, at the family swimming pool.

Preparing for National Library Week in April 1962 Mrs. Shirley Bassett with volunteers Mrs. A. W. "Galilee" Clark at the typewriter, Mrs. W. B. "Alma" Dillon and Aaron Bowman, son of Mr. and Mrs. Jay Brammer. Mrs. Dillon was a charter member of the Bassett Public Library Association and was still active when the BPLA board merged with the Blue Ridge Regional Library in 1992.

Chapter Twelve
Newspaper Clippings

Newspaper Clippings do not scan well for a book such as these, but sometimes they are treasured mementos for the families involved when someone gets in the newspaper. This chapter is presented as they are and not changed, but as the family might have them in a scrapbook.

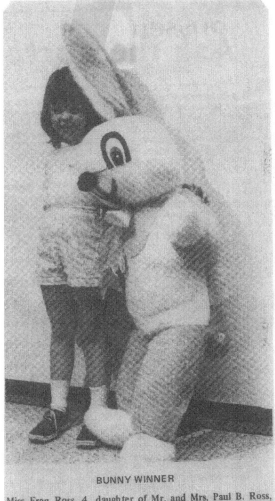

BUNNY WINNER

Miss Fran Ross, 4, daughter of Mr. and Mrs. Paul B. Ross, Bassett Heights Extension, shows off her Easter Bunny (she named him "Jim Boy"). She won Jim Boy at a drawing April 17 at Reeds 5&10 Store in Bassett. Fran has a sister Anne Marie who also likes to play with Jim Boy. Fran's grandparents are Mr. and Mrs. C.E. Clay, Ridgewood Road, Bassett.

J. D. Bassett, Sr. starts the generator for the new Bassett Table Company plant. The 1500 kilowatt generator is powered by a 2500 horse-power engine.

H. M. Penn, 73-year-old foreman of the blocking and scratch wheeling department at Bassett Mirror Co., looks over a piece of glass ready for the plate glass polishing machine. He has worked for Bassett 34 years.

A. M. Jones, Assistant Superintendent of J. D. Bassett Mfg. Co., has been with Bassett Furniture Industries for 27 years. He is shown inspecting dimension stock.

A. C. Rakestraw, assistant superintendent of Bassett Furniture Co., has been with the company 30 years. His father worked for the same firm 45 years, beginning his service in 1906.

W. B. (Buck) Heath, who started at Bassett Furniture Industries, 24 years ago, is now shipping room foreman, is shown on the packing line at Bassett Chair Co.

James E. Eanes, with 24 years service at Bassett Furniture Industries, is shown cutting curved parting rails on a band saw. Eanes has two brothers who are Bassett employees, as was their father.

Fred Belton, left, is pictured at the inspection line. He is a case fitter, has been employed at Bassett Furniture Co. 37 years. Carl Pagans, right, has completed 6 years with the company.

Three men are working at an automatic face cleaning machine at Bassett Mirror Company. Ernest Gilley, on left, has spent 7 years at Bassett. Marshall Chaney has been employed at the plant 5 years. John Wagner, right, has completed 11 years of service.

J. D. Bassett Mfg. Co. and Bassett Chair Co.

W. M. Bassett smiles as he views his dream come true ... the huge, modern table plant he so enthusiastically supervised from the planning board to completion.

Old Office Building Comes Down 2-11-65

This old office building of Bassett Furniture Industries in Bassett now is being demolished to make way for a two floor, 30,000 square foot addition to Bassett Furniture Co. A contract for the new addition is expected to be let in the near future. With the new addition Bassett Furniture Co. will be able to enlarge its Rough End Dept. and Veneer Room. The Company also will have more room for raw materials storage.

This old office building was the third General Office of Bassett Furniture Industries. The first office of the Company was on the first floor of the old bank building where the Western Auto Store is now located in Bassett. The second office was behind Bassett Furniture Co. The third office is built on part of the foundation of the Bassett Furniture Co. factory that burned in 1932. This old office was built originally in 1935. Bassett Industries occupied its new office building in 1961.

CAN YOU REMEMBER?

This was the scene in October, 1932, on the site where the present Bassett Furniture Industries office building is located as the old bedroom plant caught fire and burned. The fire was caused by spontaneous combustion, and damage was estimated at about $250,000. It was the second fire in the same plant. In 1917 some wood shavings in the plant caught fire and the building burned down completely. The plant was re-organized, and a much larger building was built in 1918.

Can You Remember?

How many of the youngsters can you identify? This is the second grade class at Bassett elementary school in 1930. Reading from left to right, starting from the bottom row, this is the best we can do in the way of identification: Madeline Coleman, W. P. Hancock, Richard Giles, Aileen Ramsey, unidentified, Tom Bullock, and Frank Bullock. Second row — Margaret Craig, Maude Cassell, Ora Stone, Harry Odell, George C. Philpott, unidentified, unidentified, Paul Turner, and William Gardner Jones. Third row — Bernice Southard, Shelburn Adkins, Christine Ingram, W. D. Eggleston, Reggie Stafford, unidentified, Beatrice Yeaman, and Raymond Ramsey. Fourth row — Rhodes Boyd, unidentified, Sadie McCraw, J. T. Ramsey, Geraldine Eggleston, Mae Law, Lee Holbrook, and T. V. Daniel.

Bassett Bulldogs? ? ?

No mistake folks...the Bassett High School Girl's basketball team, circa 1930-31, coached by Elizabeth Powell wore the "Bulldog" emblem. Mrs. Powell, current President of the Virginia Retired Teachers Association, addressed the July 2 meeting of the Henry County-Martinsville Retired Teachers Association. Seven former students, some of whom were members of the basketball team, attended the luncheon meeting. Pictured above are (front row, left to right)-Christine Joyce, Edna Bullock (deceased), Virginia Stone (deceased), Madeline Thomasson Prillaman, Inez Metz Miller, Leila Grogan, Mabel Bullock Lambert, Aileen Holbrook (deceased). Second row (left to right)-Eva Lovell Shropshire, Corrine Stoner, Alta Lovell Huley, Elizabeth Law Powell (coach) and Ada Craig Campbell.

IN 1919

Left to right are Ike Fain, Hattie Fain, and W. A. Conway. Standing in the back is Cain E. Conway. He is a former police officer at Stanleytown. Now retired after 30 years on the police force, he lives at Rt. 5, Stuart.

ALL SET FOR A SCOTTISH DANCE

Here's a look at four of the young ladies who will perform in a Scottish dance number at the Garden Gate Garden Club dance revue in Bassett, April 26. Left to right—Belinda Wright, daughter of Mr. and Mrs. R. M. Wright, Bassett; Judy Mitchell, daughter of Mr. and Mrs. Jubal Mitchell, Collinsville; Judy Park, daughter of Mrs. Glen Park, Bassett; Claudia Switzer, daughter of Mrs. John Switzer, Bassett.—(Spencer photo)

KNITTING CO. VICE-PRESIDENT

Here is Dick Hart, Sr., of Pocahontas Trail, Bassett. He is vice-president of Bassett-Walker Knitting Co., Inc., Bassett.

OLD WOODEN BRIDGE

This is the old wooden bridge in front of Bassett Memorial Methodist church. The picture was taken in the early 1920's

EASTER EGG LOCATED

These members of the Beginner Sunday School Department and Beginner Choir at Pocahontas Baptist Church found their Easter eggs early—on Wed., April 6. Shown with their collections are, from left, front row, Karen Koontz, Yvonne Koontz, Glen Koontz, Kent Pegram, Debbie Turner and Lee Ann Martin; second row, Tammy Hunter, Lisa Joyce, David Philpott, Ann Stuart Philpott, Kathy White and Graham White; third row, Mike Arendall, Kim Stone, Harrison Barnes, Mark Jones and Bernice Jones; fourth row, Lee Gale, John Jordan, Bob Joyce, Luke Jordan and Mark Jordan. Assisting in the hunt were, top row, Mrs. McGuire Philpott, Mrs. Ben Koontz, Mrs. Bill Joyce and Mrs. Yancey Arendall; standing at bottom, Mrs. Robert Martin and Mrs. C. H. Prick; not shown, Mrs. Joe Rakestraw, Mrs. Richard C. Hunter and Mrs. R. S. Jordan III. **(Journal Photo)**

Vol. 1—No. 1 Friday, October 29, 1954

History Made With The Initial Appearance Of Ben-Growl

Legislature's Authenticated Excuse Law Explained For Students, Parents

A vengeful debate about the value of these notarized excuses required by our State School Board seems to be working its way throughout our Student Body. Yet the vast majority of the debaters do not know the real significance of the new regulation they are so angrily discussing.

We know from several announcements made (when even the faculty was in the dark as to what was really implied in the regulation) that a notarized excuse is required from all students absent and all wishing to leave the campus at anytime.

But, as usual, we don't know enough because we are condemning this regulation when it is actually protecting us.

It is not required that all excuses be signed in front of a Notary Public. This is simply a convenient way for some to authenticate lunch excuses if students wish to eat in town. One notarized statement lets a student eat in town all year and frees the school of responsibility in case of an accident.

Now, signing in front of a Notary Public isn't convenient at all, so parents may call the school office between 3:00 a. m. and 4:00 p. m. and inform the principal that they have sent a written excuse. And if a telephone isn't available they may sign the excuse in front of a neighbor known to a homeroom teacher or the principal and the neighbor's signature will have the same value as the Notary Public's.

Some think the rule is a result of the recent Greenlease

Juniors Plan To Present Play

Comedy and genuine laughter are combined to set the stage as the Juniors prepare to present the hilarious three-act play, "The Little Dog Laughed," in the latter part of November.

The main character, Laurie Huntington, is portrayed by Billie Sue Gale. She is a sophomore home from college, where she is studying psychology. She psychoanalyzes all her family and friends and will keep the audience in an uproar.

Other characters are: Sidney Huntington, Laura's father, Johnny Ramsey; Martha Huntington, her mother, Peggy Miles; Wally, Laurie's younger brother, John Dyer; Joan Wood, Wally's one and only—Juanita Goodson; Ted Wood, Joan's

This Issue Marks Debut Of Printed Student Newspaper At Bassett High

Today, John D. Bassett High School adds a new page to its record of progress with an all-new student newspaper—one which, for the first time in the school's history is a printed paper. In previous years, the paper has either been mimeographed or included as part of the Bassett and Henry County Journal.

Ernestine Hill Reigns As Queen Of Homecoming

Bassett High School celebrated its annual Homecoming in a big way Friday, October 22, by defeating Dublin 14-0.

Before kickoff time the festivities began with music by the Fieldale and Bassett High School bands combined.

Members of the Homecoming Queen's Court were Opaline Woodall, Janet Mayes, Maggie

It is only fitting that a newspaper which is entirely new in appearance should have a new name as well. Ben-Growl was chosen as an appropriate name inasmuch as the school's mascot is a Bengal and the name is a contraction for "The Bengal Growls."

After being convinced for the need of a special newspaper room, Mr. Hoover agreed for the inactive wood shop to be used in this capacity. The shop will be equipped with a layout table, chairs, and a blackboard, and a much-needed filing cab-

Chapter Ten
Trent Furniture Company

The Bassett and Henry County Journal, Volume 17, Number 31, dated Thursday, June 26, 1952, devoted practically the entire eight pages of Section Two to news of Trent Furniture Company's grand opening of its newly built, modern building. The manager, Mr. William Cecil Trent, Sr., expressed a lot of appreciation to the people of Bassett, Henry, Patrick, and Franklin Counties and others in North Carolina for the success of the business since its beginning 16 years earlier.

Mr. Trent had no background in retail furniture prior to the opening of Trent Furniture Company, when he partnered with his brother-in-law, Mr. Reid Troxler. Mr. Trent and his wife, Maggie Irene Ellington Trent, had been raised in Reidsville, North Carolina. He was born March 5, 1900, to William E. and Lula Smith Trent and Irene was born March 19, 1902, to John E. and Nannie Saunders Ellington. Mr. Trent had worked as a mechanic and was foreman of the mechanical department of the Self-Bowles Chevrolet Company of Martinsville. He and his brother-in-law thought opening a furniture store would be a good idea. Their store opened in a building of the Stone Block in Bassett on the opposite side of the train tracks from this modern building. Their decision to have Cecil as manager proved to be a wonderful plan. His philosophy was that the store should do everything possible to have the customer satisfied with his purchases. The store earned the reputation of having fair prices, courteous service, and prompt delivery, so it enjoyed repeat business. In 1939, Cecil purchased his partner's interest in the company. A local general merchandise establishment, Craig and Bassett, sold some furniture, but it was not the plan of owner Pete Craig to sell furniture only – this gave Trent Furniture an opening to concentrate on selling furniture. During this time, Trent Furniture

Company participated with The Lane Company in giving the local graduating senior girls a miniature cedar chest.

Mr. Trent credited his staff with the success of the company – Virginia Davis, secretary and bookkeeper; Harold Woody, sales; E. A. Stephens, sales; and Claude Wood, truck driver.

Trent Furniture Company used the merchandising strategy of furnishing the entire home. After furniture, they offered appliances, lamps, tables, draperies, accessories, etc. This type of merchandising later became commonplace, but it was innovative in the early 1950s.

The section of the "Journal" devoted to the opening of this modern building included a page giving recognition to the companies with whom Trent Furniture Company conducted business. Mr. Trent had written these companies advising them of the planned full-page tribute and requested a copy of their letterhead to be used on that page. Many of these companies also donated door prizes for the grand opening event, which took place July 2, 3, and 5, 1952. Some of the prizes and donors were: a Universal iron donated by Hal C. Rich Company, a #210A baby bed donated by Bylo Furniture Company, rugs from Hix-Palmer Company, a night table donated by Continental Furniture Company, an electric fan donated by Radio Supply Co, a Hamilton-Beach electric mixer donated by Odell Hardware Company, two mirrors donated by Bassett Mirror Company, an aluminum roaster donated by Reeds 5 and 10, a cigarette table donated by Morris Novelty Co, a Carolina Pride Heater donated by Glascock Stove and Manufacturing Company, an Aladdin electric lamp by Aladdin Industries, a solid cedar chest donated by Southland Wood Products Company, a table donated by Kirkman Novelty Furniture Company, a mattress donated by the Mebane Company, a 50% discount on a 5-pc. suite from Stoneville Furniture Company and a few others who did not want to be named.

The opening of Trent Furniture Company in this modern building was a big event in the town. It was a modern building with a modern merchandising tactic. The building was 126 feet long, 40 feet wide, and had its warehouse in the rear of the store. This property was located on the south side of the Riverside Hotel, adjoining the property of the U.S. Government, adjacent to the post office.

Cecil and Irene had one son, Cecil, Jr., born July 12, 1943. He was 9 years old when the modern store building opened. "Little Cecil" was part of the store atmosphere from his early days and furniture sales became his career. Upon his return from active Army duty in 1965, his parents gave Cecil (Jr.) the responsibility of managing the store. They did not retire; however, instead they were active in the business until ill health curtailed their active participation.

Cecil, Jr. had found his love, Evelyn Palmer, who grew up in Pittsylvania County. They met for the first time at Cecil's Junior-Senior prom. Evelyn's cousin invited her to attend the prom and she did not want her cousin to miss out, so she agreed to go and there she met Cecil. A few months later, Cecil invited her out for the first time. They were married in 1964. They have two charming and lovely daughters, Ellie and Cathy. Evelyn, always a hard worker, proved to be a helpmate in the business world, as well as in their home Cecil continued to run Trent Furniture Company until the mid-1990s. In the meantime, business-wise Evelyn managed a complimentary store, "Used But Nice," tapping into the used, antique and collectibles world. She and Cecil frequented antique and collectibles stores, and estate sales, so this was "just up their alley." Cecil also played an active part in the operation of "Used But Nice," but Evelyn operated the store daily. They closed this store, located on Fayette Street, a block from the old Henry County Courthouse, in Martinsville in 2000 when they were needed to help with a daughter's serious health situation.

Trent Furniture Company's modern building of 1952 is still owned by the Trent Family. It has remained a part of the community housing other types of business while other companies have closed and had their buildings torn down. The building is currently being reconfigured as a place of worship.

Irene Trent died December 1, 1979. Evelyn and Cecil looked after Cecil's father before his passing on November 25, 1990. Both are interred in Roselawn Abbey, Martinsville. Regrettably, Cecil (Jr.) passed away September 21, 2009.

The Trent Furniture Company building was sold during 2011 and is now a place of worship. -- Betty Scott

W. M. Bassett on the left and on the right, R. R. Burchfield, who married Susan Hundley

Chapter Thirteen
Philpott, People, Politicians…

Fifth District Congressman Dan Daniels of Danville with Virginia Delegate A. L. Philpott with Cecil Hunt and W. C. Trent, Sr.

In September 1952, Presidential Candidate General Dwight David Eisenhower came through Bassett doing a whistle stop tour via railroad.

William Byrd on his survey of the Virginia and North Carolina boundary line first named the Smith River, a tributary of the Dan River, the Irwin (Irvine) River in 1728. Today, renamed the Smith River, it flows passively behind the Bassett Historical Center, but once it often became a raging torrent, it tried to wipe Bassett off the map several times.

Philpott Lake is a man-made lake of some 3,000 acres, which lies nestled in the rugged foothills of the Blue Ridge Mountains of Virginia. The clear body of water in its wooded setting within sight of the crest of the Blue Ridge is one of the more beautiful lakes in Virginia. Thousands of visitors from Virginia and surrounding states share its many outdoor recreational opportunities and enjoy the beauty of the lake and its surrounding forested hills.

Philpott Lake, formed by Philpott Dam, was named for the village of Philpott in Henry County, located a few miles downstream from the dam. The project was authorized by the Congress of 1944 for flood control and power generation. Construction of Philpott Dam was begun in March 1948 under the direction of the U. S. Army Corps of Engineers. By October 1951, flood control was being provided; and in October 1953, the dam and all three generators in the powerhouse were completed and in operation with the combined capacity of 14,000 kilowatts of electric power.

The Philpott Lake area, comprising nearly 7,000 acres of surrounding land, lies in Franklin, Henry, and Patrick counties of

Virginia. The project lands adjoin Fairy Stone State Park, which takes its name from the lucky or fairy stones that are found in the region. Philpott Lake with its many coves has a shoreline of more than 100 miles.

"Philpott Project" was first proposed in 1934 in a House of Representative's report on the development of the Roanoke River watershed, but was deemed economically unjustifiable. However, the Smith River Flood of October 1937 caused extensive damage, giving new significance to the project. In 1946, the Federal Power Commission called for studies that concluded a concrete gravity dam with a powerhouse at its toe was the preferred alternative. Soon after, Ralph E. Mills, Sprague and Henwood were contacted for subsurface investigations.

Construction on the Philpott Dam along the Smith River began in 1948 with operations generating hydroelectric power starting in 1953. With 3,000 acres, the lake behind the dam provides recreational opportunities on the Philpott Reservoir and at Fairy Stone State Park in Patrick County. Flood control stopped the flooding of communities downstream such as Bassett and Fieldale.

In 1948, The R.W. Mitchell Company of Winchester, Virginia was contracted to clear the banks and construct an access road from State Route 57, including a loop that would provide a spectacular overlook. In 1949, M. F. Mason of Bassett was contracted to build an Engineer's Office and W. E. Graham and Sons of Cleveland, North Carolina was contracted to construct an additional access road.

A team comprised of Bales and Rogers Corporation, Morrison-Knudsen Company and Peter Kiewit Sons' Company won the contract to construct the dam. Preparatory work began to install the cableway mixing plant and cofferdam, and the first concrete was poured on March 13, 1950.

Work was hampered by heavy rains, and on May 30, the Smith River broke through the cofferdam and inundated the excavated area. The contractor's crane and several pumps were caught in rising water. Just after the reconstruction of the cofferdam, another flash flood on September 10, 1950 inundated the area between the upstream and downstream cofferdams. However, there was no loss of equipment or time in the concrete pouring schedule. Then on January 29, 1951, a fire developed in the cableway operation house leaving the cableway system inoperable until March 12, 1951.

Installation of the penstocks began on October 2, 1950, followed by the installation of the trash rack, stop log frame, and clock-outs for the intake gate frames. The installation of the bulkhead and 5-foot diversion pipe were started in early 1951. By April of 1951, the dam was 86% complete. Ancillary work also began in early 1951, including alterations to Fairy Stone State Park Dam and cemetery relocation, which was contracted to R. R. Herndon of Smithville, Tennessee. Work to clear the Reservoir began on May 8, 1951.

The main control board, station control panel, and related equipment were furnished by Westinghouse Electric Corporation, as were the 7500 KVA main generators and one 750 KVA station service generator. Governors were furnished by Woodward Governor Company of Rockford, Illinois, and the powerhouse was constructed by J. A. Jones Construction Company of Charlotte, North Carolina. The three turbines (two 9400 Horsepower main units and one 860 Horsepower station service unit) were furnished by James Leffel and Company of Springfield, Ohio. The penstocks were furnished by Gary Steel Products Corporation of Norfolk, Virginia.

Construction of Philpott Dam cost $6,500,000, required 110,000 cubic yards of excavation, 26,000 linear feet of drilling, and 320,000 cubic yards of concrete. The reservoir behind Philpott Dam has a total storage capacity of 250,000 acre-feet. The surface area of the lake is about 4.5 square miles. The powerhouse now provides flood control for the Smith and Dan River Basin, and provides electricity to the regional power companies. Philpott Lake provides recreation for nearly 3 to 4 million visitors per year.

-- Craig "Rocky" Rockwell, Operation Manager at Philpott Dam

A. L. Philpott in his high school years.

Albert Lee Philpott, born in the northwestern part of Henry County, attended the University of Richmond receiving a Bachelor's Degree and Law Degree. After serving in World War II, the son of John Elkanah and Mary Gertrude Prillaman Philpott, he married Katherine Addison. He received his J.D. degree in 1947 from the T. C. Williams School of Law. He opened his law practice in Bassett and then was elected Commonwealth's Attorney for Henry County. In 1957, he went to the Virginia House of Delegates becoming Speaker of that body from 1980 until his death in 1991. His influence brought Patrick Henry Community College and the Virginia Museum of Natural History to the area. Highway 58 is now the A. L. Philpott Highway.

A. L. Philpott above with his mother, Mary Gertrude Prillaman Philpott and then Virginia First Lady Linda Robb. Below, Philpott with his wife, Kitty, at their home in 1985.

The sons of Albert Buchanan and Mary Elizabeth Farner Helms Philpott, Edward Jefferson, John Elkanah, and Charles Thomas Philpott had four sisters. Their father with his brothers began the community of Philpott in northwestern Henry County. Today, the dam and reservoir on the Smith River bear the family name. John was the father of A. L. Philpott.

A train heads up the Fayerdale Railroad on its way from the Philpott Station shown circa 1920. This standard gauge track went up the Smith River to present day Fairy Stone State Park, but is now under the waters of Philpott Lake. In the foreground are the tracks of the standard gauge Norfolk and Western.

The Belvie Young family in August 1946 at the Stanley Furniture Company picnic received an award for the largest family presented by President Thomas B. Stanley, who later became Governor of Virginia from 1954 until 1958. Pictured are Belvie, Vickey, Lois, Bobby, Louise, Erma, and Bill Young. Bill worked for the Miss America Pageant, judging it twice himself.

This display from the funeral of Ida Carter, born March 3, 1877, and died March 12, 1932, came to the author from several relatives including Avis Carter Turner, the granddaughter of Ida Carter. The death of a loved one often was cause for families to come together to share food and memories and due to the size of some families these became major events.

Giving credence to the saying, "Nothing runs like a Deere," is William Hodges in the Blackberry Creek section of Henry County. Agriculture was and still is an important part of the economy of the region. Tobacco farming and manufacturing once was a major force in the piedmont section of Virginia and North Carolina. Below, Martha Jane Clark and Shirley Brightwell Bassett, former librarians at Bassett.

Holding his rifle during World War I is "doughboy," M. E. Helms. Helms returned to open a shoe store in Bassett and to carry the mail. We should remember the service of these men as we approach the one hundredth anniversary of the "War to end all wars." The Bassett Historical Center contains an entire room focusing on the wars fought by this country.

Dressed in their "Sunday Finest" are Virginia Windle, Warren Gardner and Geneva Chappell, the daughters of Samuel Lucius and Nora Taylor Stone. Virginia is the author of "Some Stone Stats" and "The Way it Was in Henry County and Martinsville, Virginia" detailing the history of Henry County. Her history collection resides today in the Bassett Historical Center. Below, Mattie Lee and Ruth Ida on Wash Day 1939

On previous page, Elbert Conner Turner, born April 15, 1930, is shown on the steps of the Patrick Henry Elementary School he attended in Stanleytown. Turner worked at Stanley Furniture Company until retiring in 1994. He married Avis Carter in 1957 and had two children, Mark and Aleta. Stanleytown Elementary School shown below became the Stanleytown Recreation Center where Elbert Turner was a Boy Scout leader. Later it was a car dealership before being torn down.

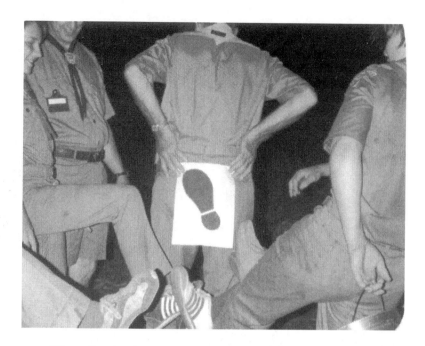

Elbert Turner forgot to bring awards to a meeting of Boy Scout Troop #74 at the Stanleytown Community Center in the 1970s. As a result, his troop, including Chuck Mason, got to kick the Scoutmaster Turner at the spot indicated on his homemade sign. Below, Elbert and Avis Turner, who for many years help plan the Bassett Heritage Festival held each September.

Bassett can claim two presidents, two college presidents. On the left is the son of Creed and Doris Maxey, Michael C. Maxey, who in 2007 became the eleventh leader of Roanoke College in Salem, Virginia. A graduate of Wake Forest, Maxey went to Bassett High School and attended Pocahontas Baptist Church. On the right is Phillip C. Stone, the son of Wilbert and Laura Stone. Phillip became the leader of Bridgewater College in 1994 after twenty-four years of private law practice. Stone owns the land where President Abraham Lincoln's family lived in the Shenandoah and holds a ceremony each year on Lincoln's birthday. Stone retired in 2010.

Lewis Bassett Stone and his wife, Mary Brown Stone. Lewis was the son of Reed Lewis and Nancy Susan Bassett Stone.

Nancy Susan Bassett Stone, wife of Reed Lewis Stone.

Craig "Rocky" Rockwell when not managing Philpott Lake does a great historical interpretation shown on the next page of William Clark of Lewis and Clark fame.

Above, the Philpott staff with Colonel. Below, the retirement of Danny Martin with wife, Susan, Craig Rockwell, and Assistant OPM Earl Wright. Danny was my 9th grade Algebra teacher, who inspired me to go to Virginia Tech.

Assistant OPM at Philpott Earl Wright. Below, the ribbon cutting for the Philpott Marina.

The Roberson Brothers, left to right, are Brown, Tyler, Lester and D. B.

Chapter Fourteen
Fon's Grocery

Emarena Rickard and Verlie Joyce at Fon's Grocery in Bassett

Fon Joyce making his famous hotdogs

The year was 1948. The Riverside Hotel housed Bassett's most formal dining establishment, passenger trains offloaded travelers at the Bassett Depot, and Bassett Furniture Industries was quickly becoming the world's largest manufacturer of wood furniture. Fon and Verlie Joyce from Bassett Forks purchased the John Hawkins residence on Main Street, located where the fire station stands today. The Joyces remodeled the home and built a grocery store on the front facade, five steps above street level. These entrepreneurs did not want to become victims of the flooding Smith River.

For the next twenty years, America's best chili slaw dogs were served from Fon's Grocery lunch counter. Talking to locals today, it is the tasty hotdogs that spur their memories about the store. Often asked for the recipe for his home made chili and sweet crispy cold slaw, Fon's reply, "How much do you need?" He preferred to whip up batches for his customers himself. So why a $0.25 hotdog is fondly remembered?

Sitting at Fon's lunch counter outfitted with the retro spinning stools was the best of Bassett. The Bassett Furniture factory workers, their bosses, the civic and community leaders, and the Bassett High School students were devoted store customers. Fon and Verlie's daughter, Jane, was nine years old when they purchased the store. During her high school years, she and many of her BHS friends congregated in the store's rear room reading movie magazines, drinking the vintage six-ounce cokes and snacking on Wise Potato Chips and hand dipped strawberry ice cream cones. The friends chatted about the BHS Bengal teams, especially the football team whose co-captain was Benny Sharpe. In 1955, Jane married the talented Benny Sharpe. The Sharpes celebrated their 50th wedding anniversary in 2005.

After returning from the U. S. Navy, Fon and Verlie's son, Bill, married Sylvia Barnes, from Martinsville. They both worked at the First National Bank of Bassett located where the Wachovia Bank operates today. The hard-working bankers would often phone in sizable lunch orders. In addition to the hotdogs, hamburgers, cheeseburgers, egg salad sandwiches, ham sandwiches and fried bologna sandwiches were featured on the menu. Take out was routine for the lunch rush.

Fon and Verlie only lived behind the store for ten years until they built a new home at Bassett Forks. The store was always opened by 5:30 am. Loyal patrons depended on Fon's for their morning coffee. Fried egg sandwiches with B and G Fruit Pies were the most popular available breakfast items. Many notable Bassett plant supervisors and local storeowners enjoyed their coffee breaks at Fon's as the fresh hot coffee was brewed until closing time. It is said that Bassett Furniture management could be caught sneaking between the factory buildings to catch a coffee break at Fon's, hoping that their absence from the plant would go unnoticed.

Fon's was also a full service grocery offering edibles for the towns 1950s - 1960s shoppers. No frozen foods, but varieties of fresh produce, deli meats, dairy products, canned goods, paper products, and sundry items were on the shelves. Hair tonic was a good seller! Grocery orders could be called into the store and the goods would be delivered to the families on the same day. Fon and Verlie frequently worked late into the evening stocking the grocery shelves, ordering the inventory, sorting the returnable glass soda bottles, and diligently cleaning the store.

The 1953 Smith River flood came dangerously close to the grocery building. Grandma Lucy Joyce was visiting and was awakened by the neighbor's hunting dogs yelping into the night. Fon and Verlie arose to find the dogs frightfully swimming in their flooded pen. This 1953 flood swept away a visiting carnival and sent farm animals floating down the river. The Joyces built their grocery store five steps above street level, the floodwaters never entered the store.

Fon and Verlie Joyce have eight grandchildren, twenty-three great grandchildren, and two great -great grandchildren. Sadly, the great grandchildren never enjoyed one of Fon's and Verlie's delicious hotdogs or viewed the Bassett Christmas parade from the cozy store, or reached into the store drink cooler for an ice cold Grapette or Nehi Orange Soda, but they will hear the stories about their Papa and Mema and the hard work they shared to serve the town of Bassett during its golden years.
-Jane Joyce Sharpe and Lynne Joyce Leonard

J and M Supermarket was another place to get groceries in Bassett. Operated by Harry and Ruby Joyce, Ada King, Barney Webb and Jim Barnes. Below, Ed Oliver, Mr. McMillan, and G. R. Holsclaw at Stanley Furniture in 1935.

Chapter Fifteen
More Folks in Bassett

Above, left to right are Mary Beth Jordan, Elsie Wright, Susie Woody, Jo Anne Philpott, Lois Lawson, Roxanne Dillon and Ruby Davis. Below, Georgia and Nellie Philpott, daugthers of Jeff and Edna Philpott.

Above, Virginia Jarrett Carter and Agnes Craig Coleman as May Queen at Bassett High School circa 1935.

Above, Leila Grogan, Trudie Fulcher Grogan, Virginia Grogan Padgett, and Marie Grogan Clay. Below, Brammer's Five and Dime employees: Marie Clay, Iris Pearson, Carlene Dodson and Sally Bet Stone circa 1939.

Above, Hida Stone, June Stone, Virginia Grogan, Erma Stone and Eleanor Jean "Cat" Stone were neighbors on Bassett Heights. Below, the M. E. Helms Family, Nancy Helms Canupp, Jack, Rachel Helms Koontz, Emma Davis Helms, and Ed Helms

Above, at a family room enjoying watermelon are Melvin Grogan, T. F. Grogan, Jr., and Marie Grogan circa 1928.

Below, Attorney Ward Armstrong represented the area in the Virginia House of Delegates for twenty years. The father of two impressive daughters, he endure the publicity that his wife, Pam, brought being the "Cover Girl" of this author's *Images of Henry County.* An avid model railroaders, Ward graduated from John D. Bassett High School in 1974 before graduating from Duke University and Richmond Law School

Above, Jim Martin made chairs in the barn behind his house in the 1920s. Located on a hill across from Valley Veneer, Martin sold his business to Bassett Furniture. Martin's wife carved and crafted each and every chair for her husbnd. Several are on display display at the Bassett Historical Center. Below, Miss Virginia 1968 with the Bassett Jaycees planting trees are Jim Franklin, Dale McGhee, Ellis Stone, Bob Clark, Paul Ross, Elbert Turner, Ron Pigg, and Bill Collins.

Good times above at the Bassett Heritage Festival and below, A. L. Philpott and John Hill Matthews

Above, Evona and Laura Adkins with a favorite teacher, Mrs. Ethel Stone Koger. Below, Debbie Hall holding baby brother, Lester.

Above, the family of Mary Bassett Ramsey. Left to right: Notan Ramsey, Ellyson, Martha Joyce Ramsey, Harriet Hundley Ramsey, Richard Giles, Mary Drucilla Ramsey, Mary Ramsey Giles, George Joyce, Lucy Belle Joyce, Daniel Helms, Nannie Helms. Below, are the Knights of Phythis, Dick Bell Lodge #155. Front row: Woodrow Bullock, Gene Turner, Frank Arendall, Hogue Craig, and Albert Stone. Second row: Gene Clay, Dennis Hall, Jim Jarrett, and C. M. Stafford. Third row: Tom Craig, Bill Shilling, Clyde Eggleston, and John Moran.

More members of the Dick Bell Lodge #155. First row: Clyde Mitchell, Maynard Mason, George Franklin, Posie Ingram, Fred Craig. Second row: Dewey Mabe, Ed Helms, J. T. Hamlin, J. P. Stafford, and Dr. E. N. Shockley. Below, Frank Bullock, a sailor from World War II.

Ann Watts Stone Hanes as May Queen at Campbell Court Elementary School in 1966 with Jimmy Mize King,

A fixture in Bassett for decades is Young's Barber Service. Below, Coy Young, John Wayne Johnson, and Sam Collins "study" the snake.

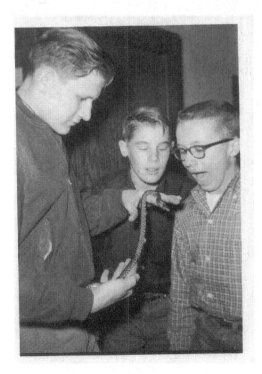

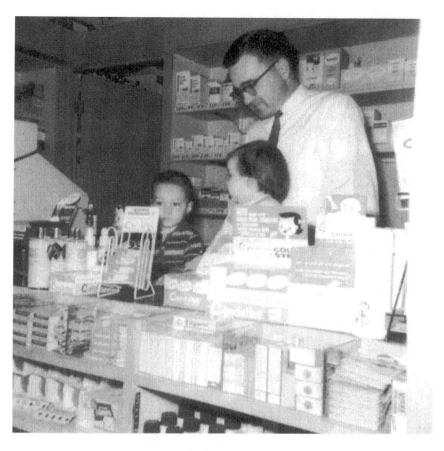

Albert Harder of Harder's Drug Store with his helpers and children, William and Susan.

Above, Steve Barton at the Bassett Area Jaycees Pancake sale. Below, Bassett Chair Company employees on July 29, 1983, celebrating their first $2,500,000 month in sales

A. F. Waleski, Principal of John D. Bassett High School. Below, ready to go to the baseball field are Gerald Martin, Jimmy Joyce, John McGhee, Jimmy Eanes, Eugene Wine, and Andy Hayes.

Still going strong at 90 years old, Mrs. Dorothy "Dot" Wickham Waleski, widow of A. F. Waleski, mother of Arthur Frank Waleski, still attends Bassett High School reunions and is loved by all in the Bassett community

Dentist Andy Lipford with wife, Lelia, with Dr. Leslie Faudree and Clarke.

Sallie Cook Booker was selected to represent Henry County in the Virginia General Assembly in 1925. In 1928, Reed Lewis Stone opposed her and lost.

Actress Angela Bassett shown with Henry Louis Gates, Jr. discovered her connections to Bassett, Virginia, on the PBS program "Finding Your Roots" with assistance from the Bassett Historical Center. Angela's African-American grandfather, William Henry Bassett, was owned in 1860 by the white Henry County native John Henry Bassett. William, born in 1846, was the son of George and Jinny Ingram of Franklin County. The reason for the different names is that many slaves took the surnames of their last owner at the end of the Civil War and such was the case of William Henry Bassett, who had been passed down through the children of James Ingram of Franklin County, who owned his parents to the Bassett family. Angela was born in New York City, but grew up in St. Petersburg, Florida.

Chapter Sixteen
From The Pages of Books

In 2010, the Henry County Heritage Book raised money for the expansion of the Bassett Historical Center.

Tom Perry's Laurel Hill Publishing released two books by Avis about her grandmother, who lived in Fayerdale, now under the lake at Fairy Stone State Park, and another about her mother, who kept a diary in the 1930s in Bassett.

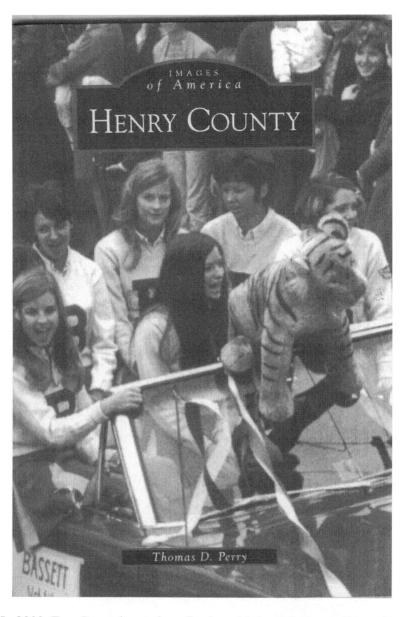

In 2009, Tom Perry donated profits from his book Images of America: Henry County, Virginia to the expansion of the Bassett Historical Center.

In the book, *Weird Virginia: Your Travel Guide to Virginia's Local Legends and Best Kept Secrets* by Jeff Bahr, Troy Taylor, and Loren Coleman, Bassett, Virginia, is the place like an elephant graveyard where all buses come to die

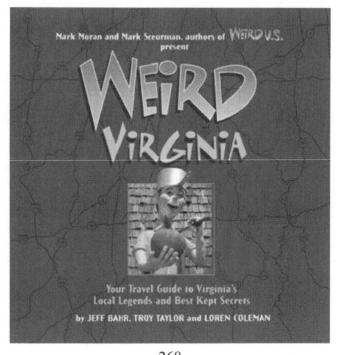

In 2014, everyone talked about was Beth Macy's *Factory Man* about John D. Bassett III, shown on the next page with the author and his fight to keep his furniture factory open in Galax, Virginia, and his family ties to Bassett, Virginia. Soon to be an HBO miniseries, produced by Tom Hanks.

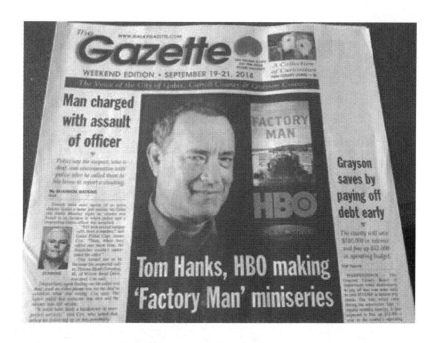

Above, John D. Bassett III signing copies of *Factory Man* at the Bassett Historical Center with Betty Scott, Shirley Philpott, and Peggy Foster. Below, his grandparents Mr. and Mrs. John D. Bassett, Sr. with Mrs. E. T. Ramsey in the Ladies Parlor at Pocahontas

John D. Bassett, Sr.

Chapter Seventeen
Photos Via Email

Lelia Grogan, Emma Brammer, Ellen Stone, and Ella Jarrett in Brammer's Five and Ten Store. Below, David Browning of Bristol, The Mayberry Deputy, came to the Bassett Heritage Festival over the years.

When I started this book, I sent out word that I wanted photos. Here are some that I got via email mainly from Anne Copeland at the Bassett Historical Center starting with Betty Josephine Philpott Martin shown above.

Philpott, Virgnia, Post Office and Store. Below, Mrs. Rosie Barnes and Mrs. Rosa Phlpott Williams at the Philpott Post Office.

Above, Red Pole Stone and Ralph Young in 1948 at the Star Barbershop. Below, Young's Barber Service in 1953.

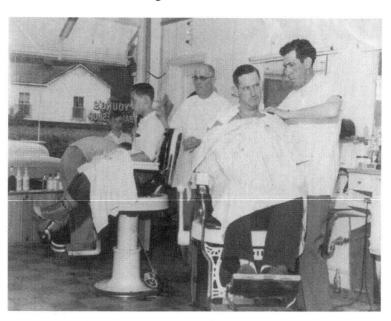

When Jo Anne Philpott is in them duplicate Perry Mason photos are always allowed.

Charles C. Bassett of Boy Scout Troop #68 of Bassett Memorial United Methodist Church.

Garden Club trip to Asheville, North Carolina, included Blandine Akers, Lucy Bassett, Jo Anne Philpott, Joy Philpott, Pat Petty, Roxane Dillon and Kitty Philpott. Below, the Claude Stone Family.

Girl Scout Junior Troop #199 from Bassett Memorial United Methodist Church with leaders Jean McClellan and Jo Anne Philpott.

Below, Christine Prillaman and Charles Philpott at their wedding with their families.

Virginia Belle Farmer and Nellie Philpott Newman.

Above, Philpott family at a Sunday lunch. Below, Rosie Barnes, Christine Philpott, and Nellie Philpott Newman and others.

Above, Adlynn Philpott Wilson. Below, Betty Josephine and Mary Adlyn Philpott, the twin daughers of Charles Philpott.

Jamie Philpott at the American Legion Horse Show in 1978. Below, Stanleytown Elementary School combined class 1-5 circa 1952.

Above, the Prillaman Family circa 1950. Below, Conley Stone, Bill Brammer, Charlie Philpott, Eddie Bassett, John Philpott and Joe Philpott.

Robert Lee Wright

LIFE OF ROBERT LEE WRIGHT

Robert Lee Wright was born January 27, 1901, in Patrick County and was one of the founding pioneers of electricity for Bassett and the surrounding counties of Henry, Patrick, and Franklin.

Robert Wright was a son of the late George Wright and the late Ruth Helms Wright. He married at the age of 16 to Lula Turperance Washburn age 14 and tried his hand at farming. Due to heavy frost damage to his crop, he left Patrick County in the early 1920's and went to work for twenty- cents an hour in the glue room at (Bassett Furniture Industries).

In 1929, he became interested in electricity and took a mail order course in electricity. To test his skills for what he had learned, he built a working model of an electric motor using only water pipes that he cut and shaped using a hacksaw. Then using two spark plugs, a spool of copper wire and window shade holders he completed the task. That model is presently displayed at EMI/HJDB in the front foyer of the Auditorium on 3289 Riverside Drive in Bassett.

Sometime during those early years, he and his brother cut many of the large beams used in the building of the table plant, using a large crosscut saw. He also worked for a short time for a company that was installing the first power lines in the Oak Level community of Henry and Franklin County. When that company considered the Bassett, Stone's Dairy and Stanleytown areas too "rural" to justify electrical services, Wright and a brother formed the "Community Electric Service". One of the first homes he brought electrical service to, was that of the late Virginia Gov. Thomas B. Stanley's Stoneleigh estate in Stanleytown.
In order to introduce electricity and convince local people that electricity would be safer than kerosene lamps; he would take a homemade alternator to local fairs and show how electricity could actually jump to parts of the human body without harm. He demonstrated he could even let the visible electrical arc jump from the device, to his fingers and even to his tongue. Robert Wright stated he thoroughly enjoyed bringing electricity to homes and relieving them of the smelly oil lamp burden. Children, he said, often would wait and watch as he and his brother readied a house for power to be turned on. "It was just like Christmas morning on those jobs while we worked late and would switch on those lights." Wright said, "I got a lot of kick out of that". He admitted raising electrical poles and hanging lines was dangerous work in the 1930s, but fortunately, his company never had a serious accident. "Blest with good fortune I never carried a man from the job to the doctor", said Wright. "The first year after we let Appalachian Power take over the lines a man

got killed", emphasizing the danger of the work. After selling the electric company to Appalachian Power, Wright operated Wrights Appliance Store in South Bassett. Many of the appliances at that time were still operated by a small gasoline engine that you cranked with a foot pedal.

While trying to operate a new business, build a home, and raise a family during the depression years he found it necessary to hunt and trap animals from the wild during the hours when most people were sleeping; thereby supplying his family with all types of meat, even including eel, muskrat, and possum. Later in the 1950s, Wright also co-owned and operated Riverside Lumber Company in Bassett often selling and trucking lumber over much of the United States. Also during that time, he began developing Sherwood Forest, Stone Plantation and Fairway Acres in Henry and Patrick counties. He then owned and operated Sherwood Forest Water Supply from 1956-1976, and supplied over 30 homes with water so that they did not have to dig their own wells. The cost of water when he turned over his lines to PSA in 1976 was $6.00 for 8,000 gallons and $0.50 for each additional thousand gallons, having never increased his rate for the 20 years he operated the water supply company.

After much prompting, he served four years on the Henry County Board of Supervisors (1956 – 60) for the Reed Creek district. During most of those years, he was a member and original trustee of Riverview Primitive Baptist Church, where he also served as deacon and clerk.

Robert Wright spent the vast majority of his adult life as a very caring and compassionate person. Telling his son, David, he had never made a lot of money, but had always tried to help himself, by helping others, and had never seen where it hurt him to do it. David witnessed this action all through his life in seeing his Dad build homes for his early widowed sisters and letting them and their growing families pay just the cost of materials whenever they could send something to apply to the cost, and not charge them any interest. He helped many people by selling them land very reasonably, when no one else would loan them money so they might one day own a home. He would then carry the note without interest until they were able to pay it off, often for years. To the frustration of his wife, he would often pass up a close parking space near a store that they needed to carry heavy bundles from, so maybe someone else might come along that might need it worse. He would often stop after getting around some obstacle along the road, and pull it away so others would not be hindered. He frowned upon cursing and riotous living. The last 20 years of his life, he spent at least one day a week visiting the sick and shut-ins at the hospital and nursing homes and never getting sick even through several flu epidemics occurred during those years.

Robert Wright died at the age of 93, on May 9, 1994, and was survived by his wife Turperance Wright after having spent 77 years of married life together at their home in Bassett, and had received congratulation statements from a large number of people including the Governor of Virginia, the Speaker of the House, and the President of the United States. –David Wright

Chapter Eighteen
Hearth and Home

The Reed L. Stone house is another residence, also known as Ithaca, which is on the National Register of Historic Places, designated in 2006.

When she is not working at her husband Robert Haley's law office or restoring old books, Cricket Coe Haley lives in the Reed L. Stone house seen on the previous page with her children Jem and Scout named for the characters in Harper Lee's *To Kill A Mockingbird*.

Eltham Manor built in 1936 is one of the places in Bassett listed on the National Register of Historic Places, designated in 1999. Designed by William Roy Wallace, the home was built by W. M. Bassett, son of John D. Bassett, Sr. Today, it is the home to Virginia and Butch Hamlet, who run Hamlet Vineyards. www.hamletvineyards.com

Hordsville, near Stanleytown, built circa 1836 by Colonel George "Rusty" Hairston after purchasing the land from Englishman John Hord.

Standing in Oak Level is the home of Isaac Jefferson "Jack" Snead. Jack and his wife, Sarah Thomas Snead, built this house and lived there with seven children: Roduskia Snead Craig, Evelyn Snead Kirby, John Harvey Snead, Jr., Henry Grady Snead, Hosea Lester Snead, Russell M. Snead, and Rachel Marsh Snead.

Stoneleigh, the home of Governor Thomas B. and Anne Pocahontas Bassett Stanley before the gardens were added to the estate.

The center garden at Stoneleigh. I lived here until my marriage. No one could have had a better example of the Art of gardening than I was priviledged to experience. My teachers were my mother, Anne Pocahontas Bassett Stanley and my grandmother, Nancy Pocahontas Hundley Bassett. I am ever grateful for their patience and guidance.

Anne Bassett Stanley Chatham

Above, Anne Pocahontas Bassett Stanley in the gardens she loved at Stoneleigh. Below, Winston Churchill, Thomas Stanley, when he was Speaker of the Virginia House of Delegates and General Dwight David Eisenhower.

Kathleen Holt of Ferrum College in 1981 when the school operated Stoneleigh. Below, the front elevation of Stoneleigh envisioned by architects Tinsley and McBroom.

The Last Chapter
The Best Little Library in Virginia

Below, Shirley Bassett worked at the Bassett Library from 1957 until 1982. She started the genealogy section that became the Bassett Historical Center.

The Historical Center is a diamond in the rough and tumble of furniture dominated Bassett. As diamonds are formed over time due to heat and pressure, so has this historical library been formed over time through the tenacity of library personnel, and through the generosity of family historians and researchers. The Center's history is tied closely with that of the Bassett Branch Library, as both were a part of the early efforts of members of the Bassett Garden Club. The early collection consistently grew through the dedicated efforts of Mrs. Effie Noland, Mrs. Shirley Bassett, Mrs. Lela Adams, and Mrs. Martha Wells Clark.

Since becoming the Bassett Historical Center in 1998, the collections have grown due to the staff and volunteers who faithfully care for the patrons and data. With over 20,000 books, 9500 family files and 3000 local history files. Collections from DuPont, Tultex, Bassett-Walker, Blue Ridge Hardware and Supply Company, and Henry County Plywood are housed here, as is the O.E. Pilson Collection. The Collection of John B. Harris is also housed here, the only African-American collection available for public access other than at the Library of Virginia. Richard Gravely compiled the "Bicentennial Collection," a collection of county records and loose papers found in the Henry County Courthouse, also housed at the Center. Researchers visit the Center from all over the United States and foreign countries as they return to where their ancestors lived or where they themselves lived years ago.

The new addition to the Bassett Historical Center completed in 2010.

The good old days at the Bassett Historical Center with my friends and staff: Pam Hollandsworth, Patricia Ross, Anne Copeland and Sam Eanes.

One of the best Civil War collections in the region is at the Bassett Historical Center with a moonshine still in the same room, the War Room.

Thanks to the efforts of individuals like Doug Belcher and Eugene Spencer, the Bassett Historical Center contains a great collection of Native American material. Below, one of the many symposiums coordinated by Tom Perry to raise money for the Bassett Historical Center.

Above, Bettie Hairstons' piano at which she played and sang for J. E. B. Stuart. Below, Tom Perry and Ashley McPeak Maguire at the Bassett Historical Center.

Ophus Eugene Pilson, an educator from Patrick County, came to live in Ridgeway and amassed a huge collection of historical and genealogical information before his death in 1999. Mr. Pilson's collection was so large that he purchased the house next door in which to keep it. Today, the Bassett Historical Center contains his collection in an entire room dedicated to it.

The Bassett Historical Center, "The Best Little Library in Virginia" is the subject of this chapter. From the *Doomsday Book* of William the Conqueror written in 1085 England to the latest research on the Goblintown Grist Mill in Patrick County, there is only one regional resource that holds both and that is the Bassett Historical Center, the best local history library in Virginia.

For years, the Historical Center was located in the back room of the regular library in the present building, but in 1998, the library moved across Highway 57 to a new facility leaving the entire building on the banks of the Smith River to history and genealogy. Today, the back room overlooking the river contains military. If you want to find your ancestor in the Civil War, there is no better room in which to begin that search. All of the Virginia and North Carolina regimental series along with the entire roster of Confederate Soldiers are present with many books and supplementary publications. You can work at a large screen computers as George Stoneman and Jubal Early peer down on you from pictures hung on the walls. If you sit in the right place, you can glance at the shelves to my favorite item, a brick from the place I preserved, J. E. B. Stuart's Birthplace.

People make a visit to the library worthwhile. The staff of the Bassett Historical Center will come through for you. Over the years of researching J. E. B. Stuart, I have traveled from West Point to Kansas to many libraries. Many years ago while reading *The Hairstons, An American Family in Black and White,* I came across a section on finding obscure material at the library. Intrigued I began to visit the library and I never cease to return to the banks of the Smith River even though it is a drive over fifty miles because it is my library home. I encourage anyone with photos to share their images for future publication to help the library. Anne Copeland summed up what any historical library should do, "The amount of material we are able to share with the public only came about because so many people were willing to share with us."

Ida Ruth Hollandsworth Carter entered her painting of the Mayflower 2 shown on the right in a 1970s art show at the Bassett Public Library that is now the Bassett Historical Center. She is with her grandson, Mark Alan Turner. The library moved across the street leaving the entire building to become the history center.

Jane Pilson at an art show held at the Bassett Public Library, now the Bassett Historical Center, in the 1970s. The liquor still is on display in the War Room that contains information on military history

Wayne Clark, assistant archaeologist with the Virginia State Library, and Richard P. Gravely, Jr. at the Koehler excavation along the Smith River in April 1976. Gravely's work on Henry County history especially archaeology pertaining to Native Peoples resides at the Library of Virginia and the University of North Carolina at Chapel Hill.

Jim and Brenda Childs and others at an archaeological site titled the "Philpott Dig" in the northern part of Bassett behind the furniture factory in October 1974. This work uncovered the skeleton of a male 28-30 years old. The Bassett Historical Center contains an entire section on Native-American history that includes books and artifacts.

The Bob White Covered Bridge in Patrick County's Woolwine community is remembered at the Bassett Historical Center with this replica built by Izzy DeJesus and presented to the library in 2009.

Below, two people who preserve the history of Bassett, Martinsville, and Henry County, Debbie Hall of Bassett, the Director of the Martinsville Henry County Heritage Center and Museum and Patricia Ross, Director of the Bassett Historical Center.

The first time I came to Bassett, Virginia, was to go out on a date. It was love that brought me back to Bassett twenty years later, a love of history. It was a book on the Hairstons that brought me to the Bassett Historical Center. Many years ago after moving back to Patrick County from Richmond, while reading *The Hairstons: A Family in Black and White*, I came across the story he tells of finding the Cohabitation List for African-Americans at the center after being told by Carl Dehart, the Reference Librarian at the Martinsville Branch of the Blue Ridge Regional Library that no such list existed. The list did and does exist at the Bassett Historical Center. This story brought me to the Bassett Historical Center after the new branch of the library moved across the street leaving the history and genealogy library the entire building. Now an $800,000 expansion has come to fruition, of which many say I am responsible for over $200,000 of that amount counting matching funds. I remember that first day using the library that became what Debbie Hall of the Martinsville Bulletin referred to in an article was "Home." I signed in and was directed to the back room where the Civil War books, Native-

American books and display and a rather large moonshine still (not operational alas) sit near windows overlooking the Smith River just a few miles downstream from the Philpott Reservoir. I chose a table on the far right and sat down. I faced the door and looked up to see high above the door a painting of J. E. B. Stuart and then out of the corner of my eye I saw a brick. Yes, a brick, but not just any brick. I looked down and noticed a card explaining the reason a brick in the War Room. It was a brick from Laurel Hill, the birthplace of James Ewell Brown Stuart, the historic site I worked to save beginning in 1990.

I remember laughing aloud when I saw the brick. The last owner of the Stuart Birthplace, George Elbert "Sug" pronounced Shug Brown, had gathered them from the site of the Stuart house and brought them into the home he shared with his wife, Icy Bowman Brown and placed them in the closet. If you visited the site in the 1960s, after spying the Virginia Historical Highway Marker placed in 1933 as the only tangible evidence that J. E. B. Stuart was born in Patrick County and stopped at the white house where the Browns lived here is what would happen. First, you would notice that on the end table there was a photo of Stuart in full uniform from the War Between the States just like he was a member of the family. The Browns were not, are not, and never will be related to J. E. Brown Stuart. He was named for his Uncle James Brown, who married Archibald Stuart's sister and Brown was not related to "Sug" and Icy. Mrs. Brown would show you her scrapbooks about the site and all the history she knew about the property. Mr. Brown would take on you a walking tour of the property and the amazing thing about him was that everything he said was dead on when the College of William and Mary did archaeology in the early 1990s. After your tour, before you left, Mr. Brown would bring out a brick from the closet and give it to you as a parting gift and a memento of your visit. I have people all over the country over the years tell me about their visits and their bricks.

Since that day I first spied the brick in the Bassett Historical Center, I have produced over thirty titles in print by the end of 2014. Coincidence, I do not think so. When you have a place that encourages your work and supports your efforts it is easy to produce. It is not a society, but a reference library that you do not check books out. It is a history library, not just a genealogical library, which people come from all over the country to use. In fact, I believe that only the racetrack and the Virginia Museum of Natural History draw more people to Henry County than the Bassett Historical Center.

It is not just a Henry County library. It is the regional history library including Patrick County. It is the Patrick County history and genealogy library. There certainly is no place in Patrick County that comes close to the collection and publications the center contains.

Dinky Railroad Exhibit at Bassett Historical Center.

In 2009, *Images of America: Henry County Virginia* came out with all the royalties from that year paid me going to the Building Fund of the Bassett Historical Center. Also, the library bought copies and the sales from these books goes to the expansion and will be matched by a matching grant from the Harvest Foundation. In other words, when you bought that book from the library you spent $22, but made nearly $44 for the library when you include the matching grant and the royalty.

If you visit the Bassett Historical Center, walk back to the War Room and look for the brick. For many years, it sat beside an old Kodak slide projector. It was the one I used for twenty years speaking about J. E. B. Stuart, raising money for the birthplace, and promoting Patrick County. There will be a history palace along the banks of the Smith River in Bassett, Virginia, where love first brought me and love of history brought me back.

Pat Ross in the O. E. Pilson Room.

Author Tom Perry with Elijah Cole Snyder overlooking Philpott Dam. As Beverly Millner stated, "If a child knows about where he came from and how important he is, that is going to do a lot for his values, his destiny in life." O. E. Pilson started me on this journey through Henry County's history and this book continues it.

Heritage is not history. It is historical memory. It is what your grandparents told you about the past, their past, your family's historical memory. Oral tradition is strong in many families and the stories in this book come from many such interactions between old and young.

History is what you can document with original letters and documents. It is footnoted and referenced. We produced a Henry County Heritage Book in 2010 to raise money for the Bassett Historical Center. This book is strong on history too. The committee wanted to produce a book strong in both areas and not the bureaucracy of how many words are in an article and how much it costs to produce a photo enlargement. This is a serious book about the history and heritage of Henry County. A group of dedicated and serious people, who have spent their lives preserving the history of their families and the county they live in, completed this book.

Many people talk about history or dress up to reenact history. While they may think that is fine, I think the best way to preserve history is in the library where it will be shared with anyone and not hoarded or archived by people with selfish motives.

I first came to Bassett, Virginia, twenty-five years ago, because I loved a girl living there. I come now for the love of history and the library that preserves this history better than any other regionally.
–Tom Perry

Continuing on the family tradition at the Bassett Historical Center, Fran Ross Snead, shown with husband Mike and border collies Bonus and Dash, is stepping into her mother's shoes as Director of "The Best Little Library in Virginia."

The next generation is assisting researchers as Cindy Hubbard Headen at the Bassett Historical Center shown with her family. Front row: Devon Headen, Jessica Wiltshire, Cindy (Hubbard) Headen, Bella, Mark Headen. Back row: Dustin Headen, Zuri and Meaghan (Osborne) Headen, Elyse and Gavin Headen.

While it might seem a bit morbid to modern tastes, this funeral wreath represents one of the older traditions. It is made of hair of the deceased in the middle and mourners around the edge.

This Chickering piano is reported to be the first piano in Henry County. Donated by Anne Wilson Covington Thompson, it once sat at Beaver Creek Plantation where Elizabeth Perkins "Bettie" Hairston played it for her cousin, James Ewell Brown "Jeb" Stuart. The portrait above the piano is the mother of Governor Thomas Stanley, Susan Walker Stanley.

Robert Harris handmade this dulcimer from Spruce, Curly Maple, Walnut and Mahogany on display at the Bassett Historical Center.

Many who did much for local history such as George Charlie Cox are remembered in the collection. Below, this photo of the Bassett High School Band Drum and Bugle Corp of 1937 donated by Posie Lee Collins, Jr., a member of the corps.

No man is an island. Many people assisted with this book. Here Kenney Kirkman and Peter Ramsey look for mistakes and information to add for this book taking a break from their many hours of researching at the Bassett Historical Center. Below, the community of Philpott is remembered.

The Bassett Historical Center collection includes a wide variety of resources including Virginia's Native-American or Indian peoples. Many displays were provided through the work of Douglas Belcher. Below, African-American's contributions are noted in the collection

The collection at the Bassett Historical Center includes many interesting items such as the cash register from Young's Barbershop in Bassett that was used for sixty years by William Young and donated by his son Coy. Below, the collection of Dr. Bing gives an idea of what serving the medical needs of Bassett was like in the twentieth century.

VMI cadet uniform of Paul Buren Ross, class of 1962, in the War Room at the Bassett Historical Center.

WWII Navy Nurse uniform of Virginia Grogan Padgett in the War Room at the Bassett Historical Center.

Post Office boxes and other items from the Philpott General Store on display at the Bassett Historical Center.

"She's the kind of person you will cross the street to meet. That smile will lift you up no matter what you were doing 5 minutes before. I first heard of Benita Lackey from my brother who had her as a teacher; she taught for many years at Bassett and Fieldale-Collinsville. He thought she was tops. Benita can entertain you with stories about her teaching days and hearing those tales, you will understand why she was a favorite teacher. She is pictured here at the Bassett Historical Center."

"This spot alongside the Bassett Historical Center's parking lot is made special in all seasons by the attentions of Snow Creek Nursery. This planting bed always looks great and never wears anything ordinary. Here are flowers planted by Snow Creek Nursery with help from Boy Scout Troop 157 and Town and Country Garden Club. Snow Creek Nursery is a family owned business that grows annual and perennial flowers, herbs, and vegetable transplants in the Snow Creek community of Franklin County. Retail and wholesale customers are welcomed."

"These days Eugene Spencer is enthusiastically promoting his Indian roots. If you visit the Bassett Historical Center, you will see his labor of love for the Indian display there contains many of his creations. A number of masks are created to be historically correct and are researched. Others are free form masks built in the manner of Indians using natural materials at hand. He is quick to tell you that local tribes did not use eagle feathers in their headdresses but used native turkey feathers instead. He is pictured below at center wearing a hand crafted headdress made of feathers and fur."

"Oh thinkin' about all our younger years
There was only you and me
We were young and wild and free..."

KISS Bassett Goodbye

As become the tradition of these photo books on Henry County communities here is KISS fan Jennifer Gregory as Peter Criss, the drummer in the band that wanted to "Rock and Roll All Night" at Bassett High School, home of another cat, a Bengal Tiger.

Index

A

Adams, 18, 21, 47, 125, 131, 171, 300, 343
Adkins, 193, 253
Akers, 5, 171, 279
Amos, 131
Anthony, 5, 25, 121
Ararat, 4
Ararat, Virginia, 339
Arendall, 122, 132, 254
Armstrong, 5, 250, 342
Ashworth,, 129
Austin, 122

B

Barnes, 112, 122, 126, 134, 242, 244, 275, 283
Barton, 259
Bassett Chair Company, 33, 38, 72, 146, 259
Bassett Chair Plant, 35
Bassett Community Market, 166
Bassett Furniture Company, 13, 31, 32, 37, 45, 46, 51, 53, 55, 57, 89, 99, 100, 111, 159, 167, 170, 177
Bassett Furnituremakers, 78
Bassett Heights, 111, 150, 248
Bassett Heritage Festival, 10, 24, 30, 100, 101, 180, 232, 252, 273
Bassett Historical Center, 10, 13, 15, 16, 17, 18, 22, 23, 26, 27, 28, 63, 68, 70, 72, 73, 84, 86, 93, 94, 114, 169, 173, 217, 228, 229, 251, 264, 265, 267, 271, 274, 299, 300, 301, 302, 303, 304, 305, 306, 307, 308, 309, 310, 312, 313, 315, 316, 317, 320, 322, 323, 324, 325, 326,327, 328, 329, 341, 342, 344, 346
Bassett Memorial Methodist Church, 139
Bassett Memorial United Methodist Church, 178, 278, 280
Bassett Mercantile Company, 145
Bassett Mirror Company, 72, 152, 160, 212
Bassett Oil Company, 144
Bassett Printing Company, 50, 181, 182
Bassett Rescue Squad, 180
Bassett Table Company, 33, 35, 152, 160
Bassett-Walker, 17, 300
Beam, 75
Beaver Creek, 16, 34, 319
Belcher, 304, 323
Belton, 170
Bengal, 112, 126, 242, 331
Bing, 11, 18, 63, 64, 65, 66, 171, 324
Bingman, 18, 36
Bi-State League, 72, 78, 79
Blackberry, 167, 169, 172, 177, 227
Blalock, 178
Blankenship, 114
Blue Ridge Hardware, 13, 143, 171, 177, 300
Bondurant, 122
Booker, 263
Bowles, 114, 115, 211
Bowman, 178, 194, 311
Boyd, 121
Brammer, 131, 194, 247, 273, 286
Brightwell, 227
Brooklyn Dodgers, 78
Brooks, 114
Brown, 16, 29, 114, 142, 234, 311, 319, 339
Browning, 273
Bryant, 75, 119
Bryson, 129
Buckner, 114
Bullock, 75, 254, 255
Burchfield, 214
Burr, 182
Burse, 111
Byrd, 6, 15, 184, 217

C

C. C. Bassett, 58, 151, 157, 159, 162, 164
Cahill, 114, 170
Calaman, 127
Campbell, 68, 113, 115, 119, 131, 256
Campbell Court, 68, 113, 115, 256

Cannaday, 18
Canupp, 248
Carnelli, 153
Carnupp, 18
Carter, 71, 75, 112, 114, 119, 120, 149, 172, 226, 231, 246, 307
Carver, 113
Cecil, 114, 167, 211, 212, 213, 215
Chatham, 57, 122
Childs, 309
Churchill, 297
Cincinnati Reds, 78
Civil Conservation Corp, 170
Civilian Conservation Corp, 155
Clark, 18, 122, 125, 127, 194, 227, 236, 251, 300, 308
Clay, 70, 73, 74, 112, 122, 125, 158, 247, 254
Coates, 121
Cobler, 114
Coleman, 75, 114, 128, 189, 246, 268
Collins, 18, 120, 122, 140, 171, 251, 257, 321
Compton, 18
Conner, 169, 231
Cooper, 119, 120, 171
Copeland, 18, 23, 26, 274, 302, 307
Corps of Engineers, 217
Covington, 319
Cox, 321
Craig, 13, 18, 32, 55, 72, 121, 128, 131, 139, 144, 149, 167, 168, 171, 172, 190, 211, 219, 236, 238, 246, 254, 255, 294
Crews, 127
Crockett, 57
Cundiff, 134
Curtis Brothers, 51

D

Dan River, 16, 22, 83, 217, 219
Daniels, 113, 119, 215
Davis, 18, 23, 26, 80, 81, 82, 114, 123, 167, 171, 212, 245, 248
Dillard, 24, 74
Dillon, 121, 182, 194, 245, 279
Dodson, 126, 247
Doss, 18, 107, 125, 342
Dove, 119, 181

Drewry Mason, 125
Duke Power, 101
DuPont, 15, 17, 300
Dyer, 18, 114, 115

E

Eanes, 18, 19, 119, 126, 260, 302
Eggleston, 18, 254
Eisenhower, 216, 297
Elgin, 92
Ellington, 211
Ellyson, 124, 254
Eltham Manor, 293
EMI, 10, 110, 116, 118, 133, 288
EMI Imaging, 10, 118

F

Farley, 88
Farmer, 30, 74, 101, 282
Faudree, 62, 262
Fayerdale, 103, 225, 266
Fayette Area Historical Initiative, 24, 68
Ferguson, 170
Ferrum College, 178, 298
Fieldale, 2, 20, 21, 28, 78, 96, 110, 113, 119, 120, 218, 328
First Baptist Church, 87, 89, 168
Fishburn, 155
Fizer, 121
Fleischman, 171
Foley, 169
Fon, 13, 241, 242, 243
Fort Trial, 12, 16
Foster, 115, 271
Franklin, 6, 70, 74, 88, 153, 190, 211, 217, 251, 255, 264, 288, 328
Fresco, 153
Frick, 128
Frith, 18, 184, 185, 341, 342
Fulcher, 5, 29, 126, 247
Fuller, 119

G

Gale, 18, 75, 126
Gates, 264
Gibson, 119, 120
Giles, 59, 254
Gourley, 121

Gravely, 15, 300, 308
Great Depression, 32, 92, 153
Great Wagon Road, 8
Greater Bassett Area Cooperative, 17, 67
Gregory, 18, 67, 331
Grogan, 70, 73, 74, 75, 125, 127, 158, 247, 248, 249, 273, 326
Gunsler, 151

H

Hairston, 15, 16, 193, 293, 319
Haley, 292
Hall, 18, 24, 25, 78, 79, 118, 126, 129, 171, 253, 254, 310, 342
Hamblen, 163
Hamlet, 293
Hamlet Vineyards, 293
Hancock, 119
Haney, 75
Hanks, 269
Harder, 168, 171, 258
Harder's Drug, 168, 171, 258
Harris, 68, 109, 300, 320
Hatcher, 119, 120
Hawkins, 242
Hayes, 119, 120, 122, 260
Headen, 18, 317
Helms, 59, 127, 128, 132, 163, 190, 224, 228, 248, 254, 255, 288
Hennis, 66
Henry County, 2, 6, 8, 9, 10, 15, 16, 17, 21, 22, 23, 26, 28, 31, 35, 51, 59, 68, 69, 74, 75, 98, 112, 113, 115, 117, 118, 167, 177, 178, 183, 211, 213, 217, 222, 224, 227, 229, 250, 263, 264, 265, 267, 289, 300, 308, 310, 312, 313, 315, 319, 331, 341, 342, 343, 344
Herman, 70, 74, 126, 183
Hickman, 128
Hill, 3, 4, 25, 121, 126, 169, 170, 172, 252, 266, 308, 311, 340, 344
Hill., 339
Hodges, 114, 227
Hogue, 13, 167, 168, 169, 170, 171, 172, 254
Holbrook, 75, 125

Hollandsworth, 71, 121, 122, 162, 302, 307
Hollyfield, 115
Holsclaw, 244
Holt, 298
Hooker, 17, 44, 58, 72, 159
Hoover, 113
Hopkins, 169
Hord, 293
Hordsville, 293
Hundley, 53, 77, 119, 120, 126, 129, 158, 163, 168, 172, 214, 254
Hunt, 215
Hunter, 55, 62, 107, 113, 168, 171
Hurd, 23
Hutcherson, 96

I

Iler, 119
Ingram, 47, 73, 121, 125, 127, 170, 171, 190, 255, 264
Irwin, 83, 217

J

J. D. Bassett, 31, 32, 35, 72, 77, 113, 146, 148, 162, 181
Jarrett, 47, 122, 128, 168, 172, 186, 246, 254, 273
Jefferson, 6, 224, 294
John D. Bassett, 5, 10, 36, 43, 53, 55, 110, 111, 112, 114, 116, 117, 118, 121, 123, 124, 125, 126, 129, 132, 133, 158, 165, 167, 193, 250, 260, 269, 271, 272, 293
John D. Bassett High School, 5, 10, 110, 112, 114, 117, 118, 121, 123, 124, 125, 126, 129, 132, 133, 165, 167, 193, 250, 260
Johnson, 127, 257
Jones, 22, 70, 74, 113, 125, 132, 219
Jordan, 245
Joyce, 5, 13, 18, 54, 59, 119, 120, 121, 122, 167, 168, 170, 172, 241, 242, 243, 244, 254, 260

K

Kelly, 64
Kirkman, 18, 212, 322

Kirkpatrick, 22
Kirks, 114
Knight, 119
Koger, 114, 134, 253
Koontz, 18, 248

L

Lackey, 95, 114, 328
Laurel Hill (Birthplace of J. E. B. Stuart), 2, 4, 338, 339
Lee Telephone Company, 87, 92
LeFeaver, 127
Lemon, 130
Leonard, 18, 192, 243
Lincoln, 233
Lindsey, 128
Lipford, 25, 121, 122, 168, 171, 262

M

Macy, 269
Maguire, 305
Malone, 33
Martin, 20, 121, 131, 170, 238, 251, 260, 274
Martinsville, 2, 16, 17, 23, 24, 32, 35, 39, 55, 58, 72, 78, 177, 178, 211, 213, 229, 242, 310, 342
Mason, 139, 182, 190, 218, 232, 255, 277
Maxey, 233
McCall, 127
McGhee, 122, 131, 171, 251, 260
McMillan, 114, 244
McPeak, 305
Miller, 76, 136
Millner, 315
Mills, 170, 218
Missionary Baptist Church, 149, 164
Mitchell, 75, 91, 112, 114, 137, 170, 171, 190, 218, 255
Mize, 256
Moore, 119, 120
Moran, 25, 121, 254
Morgan, 113
Morrison, 114, 218
Morton, 191
Mount Airy, 2, 78, 340
Mullins, 114

N

Nathan, 43, 169
National Register of Historic Places, 114, 116, 117, 291, 293
Nelson, 170
New College Institute, 17
New Hope School, 168
New York Yankees, 78, 79
Newman, 125, 282, 283, 339
Noland, 62, 300
Nolen, 125, 171, 181, 183
Nolley, 113
Norfolk & Western, 30
Norfolk and Western, 17, 96, 99, 101, 102, 103, 104, 105, 108, 161, 225
North Bassett, 42, 141, 148, 161, 169, 170, 172
Novak, 78
Nunn, 123

O

Oak Level, 115, 172, 288, 294
Ortlam, 121

P

Padgett, 25, 121, 247, 326
Palmer, 16, 212, 213
Pankovich, 121, 122
Paris., 119
Park, 31, 34, 75, 78, 93, 103, 111, 155, 170, 218, 219, 225, 266
Patrick County, 2, 15, 17, 83, 155, 218, 288, 306, 309, 310, 311, 312, 313, 339, 340, 344
Patrick County Oral History Project, 2
Patrick Henry Community College, 17, 222
Patriot Centre, 34, 35
Perry, 2, 3, 4, 25, 29, 182, 266, 267, 277, 304, 305, 315, 316, 338, 339, 340, 341, 342, 343, 344, 346
Philpott, 9, 13, 16, 17, 18, 46, 85, 86, 96, 105, 121, 122, 125, 127, 131, 132, 170, 186, 215, 217, 218, 219, 221, 222, 223, 224, 225, 236, 238, 239, 245, 252, 271, 274, 275, 277, 279, 280, 281, 282, 283, 284, 285, 286, 309, 311, 315, 322, 327

Phythis, 254
Pilson, 68, 69, 300, 306, 308, 314, 315
Plaster, 158
Plogger, 121
Plybon, 127, 171
Pocahontas Bassett Baptist Church, 27
Post Office, 33, 88, 153, 159, 162, 275, 327
Prater, 126
Price, 5, 111
Prillaman, 87, 119, 120, 151, 170, 193, 222, 223, 281, 286
Pumpkin Vine, 15
Purcell, 119, 120
Pythias, 171

Q

Quesinberry, 126
Quinn, 171

R

Rakes, 119
Ramsey, 18, 27, 32, 41, 59, 72, 111, 124, 127, 147, 160, 164, 170, 254, 271, 322
Ramseytown, 169, 170, 171, 177
Reed Creek, 114, 289
Reynolds, 163
Rich, 128, 188, 212
Riverside Hotel, 41, 75, 92, 101, 165, 166, 170, 212, 242
Rizzuto, 79
Robb, 223
Roberts, 122, 191
Robertson, 119, 140, 339, 346
Rockwell, 18, 219, 236, 238
Rodgers, 137
Roosevelt, 88, 153, 155
Ross, 18, 60, 67, 70, 73, 169, 171, 251, 302, 310, 314, 316, 325, 342
Rough and Ready Mill, 150, 192
Russell, 142, 167, 168, 294

S

Sale, 171, 177, 178
Scarborough, 164
Scott, 18, 25, 121, 172, 178, 213, 271
Sharpe, 18, 242, 243

Shockley, 61, 163, 171, 190, 255
Slaughter, 78
Smith, 9, 13, 15, 16, 17, 18, 19, 22, 28, 46, 49, 69, 71, 83, 84, 85, 86, 87, 91, 92, 93, 94, 96, 98, 101, 125, 140, 162, 168, 170, 211, 217, 218, 219, 224, 225, 242, 243, 306, 307, 308, 311, 313
Smith River, 9, 13, 15, 16, 17, 19, 22, 28, 46, 49, 71, 83, 84, 85, 86, 87, 91, 92, 93, 94, 96, 98, 101, 162, 168, 170, 217, 218, 224, 225, 242, 243, 306, 307, 308, 311, 313
Snead, 18, 122, 134, 294, 316
Snyder, 315
Southerland, 121
Spencer, 59, 191, 304, 329
St. Louis Cardinals, 78
Stafford, 18, 87, 95, 127, 134, 159, 163, 170, 190, 254, 255
Stanley, 5, 17, 21, 44, 57, 72, 121, 146, 170, 189, 225, 231, 244, 288, 295, 297, 319
Stanleytown, 9, 21, 113, 139, 231, 232, 285, 288, 293
Stegall, 18
Stephens, 212
Still, 114, 261
Stone, 18, 31, 53, 54, 73, 87, 93, 99, 103, 111, 114, 122, 126, 129, 131, 137, 138, 148, 155, 156, 159, 163, 167, 169, 170, 171, 177, 183, 211, 218, 219, 225, 229, 233, 234, 235, 247, 248, 251, 253, 254, 256, 263, 266, 273, 276, 279, 286, 288, 289, 291, 292
Stone Block, 53, 87, 138, 156, 159, 163, 169, 170, 171, 177, 211
Stoneleigh, 288, 295, 297, 298
Stoneman, 16, 121, 306, 341
Stuart, 2, 16, 17, 113, 131, 305, 306, 307, 311, 313, 319, 338, 339, 340, 342, 344
Stuart, James Ewell Brown "Jeb", 339
Superior Lines, 32, 35, 47, 72, 147, 152, 160
Swain, 132, 171

T

Taylor, 72, 169, 177, 229, 268
Teel, 25, 121
Terrilan, 121
Terry, 5, 20, 73
Thomason, 74, 114, 184
Thompson, 319
Thurston Manor, 58, 157, 164
Titus, 171
Tom Thumb, 122
Toney, 136
Train Station, 25, 29, 67, 90, 101, 166
Trent, 13, 101, 166, 167, 169, 171, 211, 212, 213, 215
Troxler, 211
Tultex, 17, 35, 300
Turner, 18, 24, 26, 62, 71, 127, 128, 183, 226, 231, 232, 251, 254, 307
Turney, 129

V

Valley Veneer, 47, 177, 251
Vaughan, 72
Virginia Machine Tool, 171, 177, 178
Virginia Machine Tool Company, 177, 178
Virginia Museum of Natural History, 16, 222, 312
Virginia Ore and Lumber Company, 103
Virginia Tech, 76, 238, 339, 346

W

Wade, 55, 74, 111, 121
Wagoner, 192
Waleski, 113, 119, 260, 261
Wallace, 126, 293
Washington, 12, 16, 51, 342
Webb, 131, 244
Weinstein, 131, 169
Wells, 18, 122, 300
Wheeler, 16
Whitaker, 75
White, 5, 78, 125, 168, 307, 309, 310
Whitlow, 18
Wickham, 261
Wike, 114
Wilkerson, 163
Williams, 25, 74, 88, 122, 127, 186, 222, 275
Wilson, 28, 74, 284, 319
Wood, 148, 172, 212
Woody, 20, 75, 170, 212, 245
World War II, 21, 53, 73, 118, 167, 170, 171, 222, 255
Wright, 10, 75, 113, 117, 118, 170, 171, 238, 239, 245, 288, 289, 290

Y

Young, 18, 114, 122, 126, 128, 191, 225, 257, 276, 324

About Thomas D. Perry

J. E. B. Stuart's biographer Emory Thomas describes Tom Perry as "a fine and generous gentleman who grew up near Laurel Hill, where Stuart grew up, has founded J. E. B. Stuart Birthplace, and attracted considerable interest in the preservation of Laurel Hill. He has started a symposium series about aspects of Stuart's life to sustain interest in Stuart beyond Ararat, Virginia." Perry holds a BA in History from Virginia Tech in 1983.

Perry started the J. E. B. Stuart Birthplace Preservation Trust, Inc. in 1990. The non-profit organization preserved 75 acres of the Stuart property including the house site where James Ewell Brown Stuart was born on February 6, 1833. Perry wrote the original eight interpretive signs about Laurel Hill's history along with the Virginia Civil War Trails sign and the new Virginia Historical Highway Marker in 2002. He spent many years researching and traveling all over the nation to find Stuart materials including two trips across the Mississippi River to visit nearly every place "Jeb" Stuart served in the United States Army (1854-1861).

Tom can be seen on Virginia Public Television's Forgotten Battlefields: The Civil War in Southwest Virginia with his mentor noted Civil War Historian Dr. James I. Robertson, Jr. Perry has begun a collection of papers relating to Stuart and Patrick County history in the Special Collections Department of the Carol M. Newman Library at Virginia Tech under the auspices of the Virginia Center For Civil War Studies.

In 2004, Perry began the Free State Of Patrick Internet History Group, which has become the largest historical organization in the area with over 500 members. It covers Patrick County Virginia and regional history. Tom produced a monthly email newsletter about regional history entitled Notes From The Free State of Patrick from his website www.freestateofpatrick.com.

Historian Thomas D. Perry is the author and publisher of over twenty books on regional history in Virginia surrounding his home county of Patrick. A Virginia Tech graduate, he studied under renowned Civil War Historian James I. "Bud" Robertson, and speaks all over the region and country. Perry's collection of papers, books, and images are housed in the Special Collection Department of the Carol M. Newman Library at Virginia Tech.

Historian Tom Perry at the site he saved, J. E. B. Stuart's Birthplace, the Laurel Hill Farm, just outside Mount Airy in Patrick County, Virginia.

Blessed are they which are persecuted for righteousness' sake: for theirs is the kingdom of heaven. Blessed are ye, when men shall revile you, and persecute you, and shall say all manner of evil against you falsely, for my sake. Rejoice, and be exceeding glad: for great is your reward in heaven: for so persecuted they the prophets which were before you.

Matthew 5: 10-12

In 2009, Perry used his book *Images of America Henry County Virginia* to raise over $25,000 for the Bassett Historical Center, "The Best Little Library in Virginia," and as editor of the Henry County Heritage Book raised another $30,000. Perry was responsible for over $200,000 of the $800,000 raised to expand the regional history library.

He is the recipient of the John E. Divine Award from the Civil War Education Association, the Hester Jackson Award from the Surry County Civil War Round Table, and the Best Article Award from the Society of North Carolina Historians for his article on Stoneman's Raid in 2008. In 2010, he received acknowledgement from the Bassett Public Library Association for his work to expand the Bassett Historical Center and was named Henry County Virginia Man of the Year by www.myhenrycounty.com. Perry also recently received the National Society of the Daughters of the American Revolution Community Service Award from the Patrick Henry Chapter Daughters of the American Revolution.

Below, Dot Powell, Tom Perry and Joan Frith at the Patrick Henry Chapter of the National Society of the Daughters of the American Revolution.

Tom Perry Received National Community Service Award approved by the National Society of the Daughters of the American Revolution in Washington, D. C. The remarks of Regent Joan Frith at the ceremony On February 9, 2011, at the Dutch Inn in Collinsville, Virginia. "The Patrick Henry Daughters of the American Revolution would like to present the National Society of the Daughters of the American Revolution Community Service Award today. This award recognizes worthy residents from a variety of walks of life for their unpaid voluntary achievements. The recipient must have contributed to the community in an outstanding manner. It also must be approved by the national chairman. Our Community Service Chairman, Dot Powell, submitted letters of recommendation and supporting documentation from Patricia Ross, Director of the Bassett Historical Center, Deborah Hall, Director of the Martinsville Henry County Historical Society, Andy Doss, past president of the Sons of the American Revolution and Delegate Ward Armstrong.

Thomas David Perry has devoted much of his life to the preservation of history. He founded the J. E. B. Stuart Birthplace Preservation Trust. He is the author of 15 books on local and regional history. A portion of the proceeds have been donated to a number of local organizations. He donated all the royalties from the sale of his book, Images of America: Henry County, Virginia to the Bassett Historical Center raising over $25,000 for its building campaign. He is chairperson of the Henry County Virginia Heritage book committee and proceeds of this book also going to the building fund for the Bassett Historical Center. His donations to schools, museums and communities have been numerous. He has spent the last 25 years of his life preserving and sharing the history of our region and Nation.

We are honored to present the National Society Daughters of the American Revolution Community Service Award to Thomas David Perry."

Elva Adams wrote on her website www.myhenrycounty.com

"I remember when I didn't know Tom Perry. One day I was discussing local history aficionados and collectors with someone close to that venue. And that person said, "Tom Perry is a good guy". Our association now has evolved to the Henry County Historical Book Project. Early on, someone asked a question of committee chair Tom about how the book would be laid out. It was a sticky question and Tom answered it by saying "We will do it this way because I'm the Law." You see Tom lives in Ararat, which is very close to Mayberry, NC, the home of that most famous sheriff Andy Griffith. So that very afternoon I placed a Photoshop star on Tom's author picture here. Tom liked my star so much that he bought himself a Mayberry Sheriff's badge to wear to meetings. Well it is a feisty group and a sheriff really is sometimes necessary. ;)

"Many talk the talk. This one talks and walks... and drives. In the last few years he has driven hundreds of miles from Ararat to Bassett in support of the "Best Little Library in Virginia", the Bassett Historical Center. Thank you Patrick County for sending him our way! His efforts in raising funds for the Bassett Historical Center go unmatched by anyone. Each spring he conducts a History Seminar and brings in interesting and nationally known speakers. He publishes books (Laurel Hill Publishing) on history and if you buy your copies at the Bassett Historical Center, they receive all the proceeds. He has most recently led a group of Henry County residents in completing the Henry County Heritage Book in less than one year. His life is a mission: J.E.B. Stuart, the Bassett Historical Center, and the presentation of History itself. We are lucky to have him in our midst. www.myhenrycounty.com named Tom Perry 2010 Man of the Year."

Thank You Thomas Perry!

I would like to take this moment to Thank Thomas Perry for all that he has done for the Bassett Historical Center and the promotion of regional and local history. Tom has tirelessly devoted his efforts and resources in support of the Bassett Historical Center and many other deserving organizations. The Patrick Henry Chapter of the DAR presented Tom with their Community Service Award in February 2011. The DAR chapter in turn received a third place award from the State for their nomination of Tom for Community Service. The Col. George Waller chapter of the SAR presented Tom with their Bronze Good Citizenship award in 2005. Tom's mission has always been the education and promotion of history. He started the J.E.B. Stuart Birthplace Preservation Trust, Inc. in 1990 and the online Free State of Patrick website on 2004, which has grown to over 500 members.

Tom has produced the Laurel Hill Teacher's Guide for educators and the Laurel Hill Reference Guide for groups. Additionally, Tom speaks with students at several local schools and colleges. Tom has his collection of papers relating to J.E.B. Stuart and Patrick County history at his alma mater Virginia Tech, in the Special Collections Department of the Carol M. Newman Library under the auspices of the Virginia Center for Civil War Studies. He has donated his collection of over 14,000 photos and images to the Bassett Historical Center and the Mount Airy Museum of Regional History. Tom was instrumental in developing the Historical Symposiums held to benefit the Bassett Historical Center's Building Fund, as well as, encouraging James I. Robertson, Jr. to be a speaker. He has presented multiple "First Saturdays" programs annually, on various local topics of local history over the past five years. He served as editor of the Henry County Heritage Book and led the group of volunteers to complete the book within a year. All proceeds from the Heritage Book and Tom's "Arcadia Publishing's Henry County, VA book went to the Bassett Historical Center's Building Fund to help raise over $50,000 for the expansion of the building. Tom participated in the Big Read in October, holding the final event for Poe on Halloween at the Bassett Train Depot. Tom has gone above and beyond for the promotion of local and regional history and deserves a huge Thank You for all he has done for the Blue Ridge Regional Library system and the Bassett Historical Center. The deeds listed above are just a sampling Tom's outstanding contributions. We are truly fortunate to call Thomas Perry our friend!

Ruby Davis, Editor

James I. "Bud" Robertson of Virginia Tech came to Bassett to assist in fund raising for the Bassett Historical Center. A mentor of Tom Perry, Robertson was serious in his talk and funny standing on a chair to be taller than his former student.

Made in the USA
Charleston, SC
22 June 2015